Brain Teasers

Including the Tricky Twenty

by Kiran Srinivas

Robert D. Reed Publishers
San Francisco

Robert D. Reed Publishers
750 La Playa Street, Suite 647
San Francisco, CA 94121
Phone: 650/994-6570 • Fax: 650/994-6579
E-mail: 4bobreed@msn.com
Web site: www.rdrpublishers.com

Designed and typeset by Katherine Hyde, Hyde Publishing Services
Cover designed by Julia A. Gaskill at Graphics Plus

ISBN 1-885003-99-4

Library of Congress Control Number: 2001117666

Produced and Printed in the United States of America

FSC
Mixed Sources
Product group from well-managed
forests and other controlled sources

Cert no. SW-COC-002283
www.fsc.org
© 1996 Forest Stewardship Council

Contents

About the Author

Kiran Srinivas, 26, is a huge fan of brain teasers and other mental puzzles. He currently works at an asset-management firm in New York City. He previously worked on Wall Street as an investment banker and as a futures/derivatives trader. He holds an MBA from Harvard Business School and a BA in Economics from Stanford University.

In his spare time, Kiran enjoys playing sports (especially football and basketball), spending time with family and friends, reading, dancing, and playing cards and chess.

Introduction

To succeed in life, you must "think outside the box." This cliché phrase is used to describe creative, non-standard approaches to problem solving. The value of such thinking is enormous. In the Trojan War, the clever Greeks created the Trojan Horse. Without this innovation, they would not have been able to enter Troy and rescue their princess Helen. More recently, clever thinkers have come up with ideas such as free Internet e-mail accounts, an online auction site, and effective viral marketing tactics.

But how does one learn to "think outside the box"? Unfortunately, there is no simple answer. However, I do believe that you can significantly improve your thinking abilities. This book will force you to think hard and to think in ways you never have before. By sheer practice, you will increase your ability to think creatively.

Spend ample time on each puzzle. Many of the puzzles (especially the Tricky Twenty) will take hours, if not days, to solve, so stay focused and upbeat. Do not look at the solutions right away. If you must peek, only look at the answer to each puzzle; do not read the attached logic. Be encouraged that a middle-school education is sufficient to answer almost all of the puzzles.

There are many interview puzzles in this book. If you plan to interview at an investment bank, consulting firm, high-tech firm, or in any other related field, make sure to absorb this book fully—it can be the deciding factor in getting that offer.

Good luck!

Part 1

Puzzles

Brain Teaser #1

Each equation below contains the initials of words. Furnish the missing words to solve each equation.

For example, 60 = M in an H would be 60 = Minutes in an Hour.

26 = L of the A

7 = W of the A W

1001 = A N

12 = S of the Z

54 = C in a D (with the J)

9 = P in the S S

88 = P K

13 = S on the A F

18 = H on a G C

32 = D F at which W F

8 = S on a S S

3 = B M (S H T R)

90 = D in a R A

24 = H in a D

57 = H V

11 = P on a F T

1000 = W that a P is W

29 = D in F in a L Y

200 = D for P G in M

5 = D in a Z C

Brain Teaser #2

What is the maximum value of change that you can have in U.S. coins (pennies, nickels, dimes, quarters, and half-dollars) without being able to give exact change for a U.S. dollar bill?

This question is looking for the maximum monetary value of the coins, not the maximum number of coins.

Brain Teaser #3

A high school has 1,000 students and it has 1,000 lockers in its main corridor. All of the lockers are initially open.

The first student walks down the corridor and changes the position (open/close) of each locker. In his case, he closes all of the lockers since they are all open. Then the second student walks down the corridor and changes the position of every second locker (in his case he will open all of the even-numbered lockers). Then the third student walks down the corridor and changes the position of every third locker (in his case he opens some and closes some). Then the fourth student walks down and changes the position of every fourth locker, etc. How many lockers are closed after the one-thousandth student is done? (Remember that the last student changes the position of every one-thousandth locker, which means he only changes the position of the last locker.)

Brain Teaser #4

Part 1: Is it possible to make five squares with twelve equal-sized toothpicks? If so, how? If not, why not?

Part 2: Is it possible to make four equilateral triangles with six equal-sized toothpicks? If so, how? If not, why not?

Brain Teaser #5

In southern Egypt, there are magical lily ponds. On these ponds, each flower doubles every night. For example, if a pond has one flower on a certain day, the next day there will be two flowers (both the same size as the original flower).

On March 1, you place a single flower on an empty magical pond. On the last day of the month, March 31, you return to find the pond's entire surface 100% perfectly filled with flowers. What was the first day on which the pond's surface was at least 30% covered with lily flowers?

Brain Teaser #6

Suppose you are on a boat in the middle of a lake. On the boat, you have a very heavy lead anchor. If you were to drop the anchor into the lake, would the water level rise, fall, or stay the same? Why?

Brain Teaser #7

You have twenty-one socks in a drawer. Six of them are green, seven of them are yellow, and the remaining eight are red. It is dark so you can't see what color sock you pull out. What is the minimum number of socks you need to pull out of the drawer to ensure that you have a matching pair of socks?

Brain Teaser #8

When a clock is at 3:15, what is the separation in degrees between the hour hand and the minute hand?

Brain Teaser #9

You have a gigantic 10 × 10 × 10 cube made up of 1000 smaller 1 × 1 × 1 cubes (pictured below). How many of the smaller 1 × 1 × 1 cubes can you see on the surface of the giant cube?

You are permitted to flip the giant cube so you can see all of the six sides, but you can't break it open.

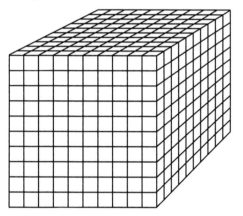

Brain Teaser #10

Part 1: Name a word in the English language that has the letters *gnt* in that exact order right next to each other (i.e., no letters between *gnt*).

Part 2: Name a word in the English language that contains all five vowels and the letter *y* (often considered the sixth vowel) in alphabetical order (i.e. the *a* precedes the *e*, the *e* precedes the *i*, etc). There can obviously be consonants in between the vowels.

Part 3: Name a word in the English language that has three consecutive double letters. A double letter occurs when the same letter appears right next to itself. (For example, *balloon* has two consecutive double letters, and *Mississippi* has three non-consecutive double letters.)

Brain Teaser #11

A bare room has a table with three light bulbs on it. You are outside the room, where there are three switches, each of which is connected to one of the three light bulbs. At first, all of the lights are turned off and all of the switches are in the off position. The door to the room is closed. You may do anything with the switches. You then must open the door and enter the room. You may then do anything inside the room. Once you enter the room, you can't exit again. Your task is to determine which switch is connected to which bulb. Can you do it?

If so, how? If not, why not?

Brain Teaser #12

Larry, Curly, and Mo spend a night together at a roadside motel. When they enter, the clerk charges them $30 for the room. Each pulls out a $10 bill and pays the clerk. The men then go to their room. When the manager returns to the front desk, he realizes the clerk has overcharged the three guests since a room only costs $25. The manager tells the clerk to return $5 to the three guests.

In the elevator, the clerk realizes that he can't evenly split $5 among three people, so he decides to give each of the three guests $1 each and illegally pocket the other $2. Thus, when the clerk arrives at the guests' room, he tells the three they have been overcharged by $3 and he hands Larry, Curly, and Mo each $1.

Now, in the end, Larry, Curly, and Mo each have paid $9. This is a subtotal of $27. The clerk has $2. This brings the total to $29. However, Larry, Curly, and Mo initially paid $30. What happened to that last "missing" dollar?

Brain Teaser #13

Read this sentence aloud:

FINISHED FILES ARE THE RE-
SULT OF YEARS OF SCIENTIF-
IC STUDY COMBINED WITH
THE EXPERIENCE OF YEARS.

Now go back and quickly count the Fs in the sentence. Count them only once. How many Fs are in the sentence?

Brain Teaser #14

You have a jar that has 10 liters of pure apple juice and a mug that has 10 liters of pure orange juice. You take 1 liter of the apple juice from the jar and pour it into the mug of orange juice. You stir up the mug (which is now mostly orange juice, diluted by the 1 liter of apple juice). You then take 1 liter from the mug and pour it back into the jar of apple juice. You now have diluted both containers with the opposite liquids. Which container is more diluted? In other words, does the jar have more orange juice or does the mug have more apple juice?

Brain Teaser #15

A small town in France has 207 residents. Each summer the town has a tennis tournament in which everyone participates. The townspeople are told to keep playing until they lose a match. Instead of scheduling a tournament bracket, everyone is told to walk around town asking each other to find out who has yet to lose a match. When someone finds someone else who hasn't lost yet, the two play a match. This continues until there is only one person who hasn't lost a match, and that person is crowned the town champion.

What is the minimum number of matches that could theoretically be played in the tournament in any given year? What is the maximum number of matches that could theoretically be played in any given year?

Brain Teaser #16

Part 1: Four U.S. states have the word "City" in their capital. Name them.

Part 2: Four U.S. state capitals start with the same letter as the state. Name them.

Brain Teaser #17

You have nine marbles. Eight are normal weight and the other one is slightly lighter. You also have a balance scale. What is the minimum number of times that you need to use the balance scale to determine which is the lighter marble?

Brain Teaser #18

Take all the integers from 1 to 1,000,000. What is the sum of all of the *digits* that are required to write down all of these numbers?

Time limit: 5 minutes.

Brain Teaser #19

Yesterday you drove from Chicago to Toledo at 30 mph. Today, you are going to return to Chicago from Toledo. You want to average 60 mph for your entire round-trip. At what speed do you need to drive on your return trip so that you average your desired 60 mph for the overall round-trip?

Brain Teaser #20

You are placed in a jail cell with two identical doors, each with a guard standing next to it. One door leads to freedom, the other to a den of man-eating lions. One guard always tells the truth, the other always lies. You have to select a door and walk out, but before doing so you are allowed to ask one question (which can't have multiple subparts) to either of the two guards. You have no way to determine which guard tells the truth and which one lies. Can you ask a question to guarantee an escape to freedom?

If so, how? If not, why not?

Brain Teaser #21

You buy a square plot of land that measures 1 mile by 1 mile. You want to land your private plane on your property, but you know that you need a runway of at least 1.25 miles to land a plane. Luckily, you also own a tractor that can tilt land at a 10% gradient at any given point. Can you create a runway that will allow you to land your plane?

Brain Teaser #22

Your sister drops a red ball from 1 meter off the ground. On every successive bounce, the ball bounces back into the air one-half the distance from its previous peak. So the ball initially bounces up 0.5 meters, then falls back down, then bounces up 0.25 meters, etc. This continues forever. What is the total distance that the ball travels?

Brain Teaser #23

Pick a number from 1 to 10.
Multiply the number by 3.
Sum the digits of the number (for example, 14 → 1 + 4 → 5 or 9 → 9).
Subtract 6.
Square the number.
Add 4.
Sum the digits of the number (for example, 14 → 1 + 4 → 5 or 9 → 9).
Map the number to a letter of the alphabet (1 = A, 2 = B, 3 = C, 4 = D, 5 = E,
   etc).
Think of a country whose name starts with this letter.
Think of the second letter of this country's name.
Think of an animal whose name starts with this second letter.
Think of the color of this animal.

Look at the solution.

Brain Teaser #24

After returning from a violent battle, the army general surveys his troops
and realizes that his men are severely wounded. In particular, 70% of the
soldiers have lost an arm, 75% have lost a leg, 80% have lost an ear, and
85% have lost an eye. What is the minimum percentage of troops that have
lost all four body parts?

Brain Teaser #25

Part 1: Suppose the probability of having a boy is 50% and that of having a girl is 50%. You know a couple with two children. You know that the older child is a boy. What is the probability that the younger child is also a boy?

Part 2: Suppose the probability of having a boy is 50% and that of having a girl is 50%. You know a couple with two children. You know that one of the children is a boy. What is the probability that the other child is also a boy?

Brain Teaser #26

In bowling, can you bowl under 100 while having eight strikes and no gutter balls?

If so, how? If not, why not?

Brain Teaser #27

You leave Atlanta at 8 AM on Sunday morning and arrive in Detroit at 8 PM that same day. You take breaks on the 12-hour journey, and you change speeds throughout the trip due to traffic, weather, and fatigue. The next Sunday you leave Detroit at 8 AM and return home to Atlanta at 8 PM that night (again, you take breaks and change speeds on your journey).

Is it possible that you are never at the exact same location at the exact same time on the two Sundays?

If so, how? If not, why not?

Brain Teaser #28

Billy offers you the chance to play a game in which you will definitely win some money. You greedily ask for details. He says that you flip a fair coin until it lands on tails. If you flip a tail on your first flip, you get $1. If you get one head, then a tail, you get $2. If you get two heads, then a tail, you get $4. If you get three heads, then a tail, you get $8. This continues forever, so every successive head doubles your winnings. (A streak of seven initial heads before the first tail wins you $128.)

You are guaranteed to win money, so Billy demands you pay a fee to play the game. Assuming you are risk-neutral and only willing to pay the expected value of your winnings, what should you pay to play? (Expected value of winnings is the mathematical term for the average amount you expect to win.)

Brain Teaser #29

If four hens can lay four eggs in four minutes, how many eggs can eight hens lay in eight minutes?

Brain Teaser #30

What is the minimum number of people needed in a room to have over 50% probability that there are two people with the same birthday?

For the purpose of this riddle, assume the year has 365 days (no February 29).

Brain Teaser #31

You are thrown in jail. The jury decides that you are going to play a game to determine your fate. You are given two empty boxes and twenty balls. Ten of the balls are white, and the other ten are black. You are allowed to place the balls in the two boxes in any way you want. After you do so, the warden will randomly select one of the two boxes, stick his hand into that box, and then randomly select a ball. If the ball is white, you are acquitted; if the ball is black, you are killed. If the box the warden initially selects has no balls in it (which could happen if you placed zero balls in the first box and all twenty in the second box), the warden will default to the other box and randomly select a ball from there.

What is your maximum probability of survival? How?

Brain Teaser #32

You have $100 in your bank account. You make six withdrawals totaling $100. Here is the record of those withdrawals, along with the remaining balances:

Withdrawal Amount	Remaining Balance
$50	$50
25	25
10	15
8	7
5	2
2	0
$100	$99

You are somewhat confused. The withdrawals sum up to $100, as you expected. But the balances only sum up to $99. How is this possible? Where is the last dollar?

Brain Teaser #33

Paul is twenty years old in 1980, but only fifteen years old in 1985. Is this possible?

If so, how? If not, why not?

Brain Teaser #34

Why are 1998 quarters worth more than 1976 quarters? And approximately how much more?

Brain Teaser #35

Can you place eight queens on a chessboard (pictured below) so that none of them is in position to capture another queen?

If so, how? If not, why not?

In chess, a queen can move as many squares as the board allows either vertically, horizontally, or diagonally, and it can capture any piece in its path in any of these directions.

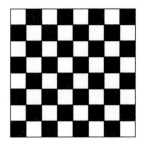

Brain Teaser #36

Barry, Craig, and Dave are walking back to the barracks. Early in the walk, Barry takes out a loaf of bread, splits it into three pieces, and each soldier eats a piece. Later, Craig takes out a loaf of bread, splits it into three pieces, and each soldier eats a piece. Later, Dave says he has no bread or money with him. So Barry takes out another loaf of bread, splits it into three pieces, and each soldier eats a piece.

Assume each loaf of bread costs $3. When they get back to the barracks, what is the easiest way for the soldiers to settle all of their debts?

Brain Teaser #37

Two brothers, Tim and Al, sell strawberries in Florida. Every morning Tim and Al go to the fields and each collects 30 strawberries. In the afternoon, they both set up a booth and sell their goods. Tim sells his strawberries at 2 for $1 and makes $15 every day. Al sells his strawberries at 3 for $1 and makes $10 every day. At night, they take the combined $25 and buy dinner for themselves and their father.

One day Tim and Al decide that they should combine their strawberry sales, which would allow one of them to take off from work each afternoon. Since Tim sells 2 for $1 and Al sells 3 for $1, they decide to sell 5 strawberries for $2. The first day, Tim agrees to work the afternoon. After Tim and Al each collect 30 strawberries in the morning, Al goes home to relax. There are a total of 60 strawberries, which Tim sells at 5 for $2. He makes 12 sales at $2 each for a total of $24. This is $1 short of the $25 that Tim and Al made when selling strawberries separately.

Everyone is perplexed—no one can figure where the missing dollar is. Did Tim steal it? What happened?

Brain Teaser #38

When you bet on a football game, you wager $11 in the hope of winning $10. So, every time you win, you collect $10, but when you lose, you pay $11. With these odds, how often do you have to win to break even financially?

Brain Teaser #39

You have some rope. You cut off a piece to fit snugly around the earth's equator. The rope does not have any slack. You then take that piece of rope and add another 12 inches to it. You now place the new piece of rope around the equator; this time there is some space between the rope and the earth's surface, since this new rope is 12 inches longer than the earth's equator. You place the rope around the equator such that the space between the surface of the earth and the rope is evenly distributed around the whole equator.

Which of the following objects can fit through that space: a car, a mouse, or a hydrogen atom?

Suppose you take a basketball (instead of the earth) and repeat the experiment (i.e., adding 12 inches to a rope after it fits snugly around the basketball). Now, which of the three objects would fit between the rope and the basketball?

Brain Teaser #40

You have an empty 5-liter vessel and an empty 7-liter vessel. You need to measure out exactly 6 liters of water. You have a running water faucet (with an infinite amount of water in it). What is the minimum number of moves required to get exactly 6 liters of water? (Here a move is defined as either (a) filling up a vessel, (b) dumping water out of a vessel, or (c) transporting water from one vessel to another.)

Now assume that you don't care about the number of moves, but rather are interested in the amount of water used. What is the minimum amount of water needed from the running faucet?

Brain Teaser #41

Why are manhole covers circular?

Brain Teaser #42

Tom and Jill play a simple game in which they alternately flip a coin. Whoever flips a head first wins. Tom flips first. (If he flips a head, he wins and the game is over. Otherwise, Jill flips, etc.)

What is the probability that Tom wins?

Brain Teaser #43

Larry's birthday is today. He tells me that Jim, his older twin brother, has a birthday coming up in two days. Is this possible? Or is he lying?

Let me clarify two items. First, Larry is a twin to Jim (so don't assume that Larry is much younger than Jim and that Jim has another twin brother). Second, assume younger means "born after" and older means "born before."

Brain Teaser #44

At 9 AM, Train ABC leaves Los Angeles and heads north toward San Francisco at 40 mph. At the same time, Train XYZ leaves San Francisco and heads south toward Los Angeles at 60 mph. San Francisco is 600 miles north of Los Angeles. At 9 AM a bee also leaves Los Angeles and heads toward San Francisco, traveling along the railroad tracks at 75 mph. Once the bee reaches Train XYZ, it turns around and heads back toward Los Angeles and toward Train ABC (still at 75 mph). Once it gets back to Train ABC, the bee turns around again. The bee keeps doing this until the trains crash into each other.

Eventually, somewhere between Los Angeles and San Francisco, the trains do crash into each other and the bee is killed in the collision. How many total miles does the bee travel before its death?

Brain Teaser #45

Part 1: A total of five teams in professional baseball (MLB), professional football (NFL), and professional basketball (NBA) have nicknames that do not end in the letter *s*. Name them.

Part 2: A total of five nicknames are used by two different franchises in professional baseball (MLB), professional football (NFL), professional basketball (NBA), and professional hockey (NHL). Name them.

Brain Teaser # 46

If the puzzle you solved before you solved the puzzle you solved after you solved the puzzle you solved before you solved this one was harder than the puzzle you solved after you solved the puzzle you solved before you solved this one, was the puzzle you solved before you solved this one harder than this one?

Brain Teaser #47

A baseball pitcher throws a strike 50% of the time and a ball 50% of the time. He faces a batter who does not swing on any pitch. What is the probability that the pitcher strikes out the batter?

A pitcher strikes out a batter if he throws three strikes before throwing four balls.

Brain Teaser #48

What is the beginning of eternity? The end of time and space? The beginning of every end? And the end of every place?

Brain Teaser #49

Oliver, Olga, and Oscar each have two different hobbies. No one has a hobby that someone else has. Their hobbies are: golfer, swimmer, biker, skateboarder, sailor, and scuba diver. Each character in the following statements represents a distinct person.

1   The golfer and the swimmer are both taller than Oliver.
2   The sailor beat the skateboarder in chess yesterday.
3   The biker and skateboarder eat lunch together every Wednesday.
4   The swimmer and the sailor are both vegetarian.
5   The sailor is smarter than both Olga and Oscar.
6   The golfer and Olga are husband and wife.

Match each person to his or her hobbies.

Brain Teaser #50

Gary and Barry race in a 50-yard dash. Gary wins by 5 yards. They decide to race again, and to make things more equal, Gary starts 5 yards behind the original start line. Who wins the second race?

Assume that both runners maintain the same speeds in the second race as they previously ran in the first race.

Tricky Twenty #1

There are five pirates. All are intelligent and greedy. They have 100 gold coins to split among themselves. The pirates have seniority in the following order: Pirate A, Pirate B, Pirate C, Pirate D, and Pirate E. The pirates all know the rules of the game, which are: Pirate A initially makes a suggestion about how to split up the coins (for example, he could say Pirate A gets 50, Pirate B gets 10, Pirate C gets 10, Pirate D gets 25, and Pirate E gets 5). Then they all vote on the suggestion (including Pirate A). If a majority votes for it or if there is a tie (you will shortly see how there can be a tie), the suggestion is approved and the game ends. Otherwise, Pirate A is thrown overboard to his death. If Pirate A dies, then Pirate B becomes the most senior pirate, so he now gets to make an allocation suggestion (for example, he could say all four remaining pirates each get 25 coins). They all vote (including Pirate B), and if a majority votes for it or if there is a tie, the suggestion is approved and the game ends. Otherwise, Pirate B gets thrown overboard to his death and Pirate C becomes the most senior pirate, etc.

Knowing that all of the pirates are intelligent and greedy, what happens?

There is only one stable, equilibrium solution.

Tricky Twenty #2

Four people want to cross a bridge. It is nighttime, so they need a flashlight while on the bridge. The bridge can only support the weight of two people at any given time. The group has only one flashlight. When two people are on the bridge, they must walk at the slower person's speed, because both people need to be next to the flashlight. The flashlight can't be thrown, it must always be walked back and forth from one side of the bridge to the other.

Person A takes 1 minute to cross the bridge. Person B takes 2 minutes to cross, Person C takes 5 minutes to cross, and Person D takes 10 minutes to cross. What is the minimum amount of time to get all four people across the bridge?

Tricky Twenty #3

My parents attended a dinner party where they were one of the 22 couples present. At the beginning of the party, people were wandering around introducing themselves to each other, and sometimes people shook hands with one another. No one shook hands with his or her own hand, no one shook hands with his or her spouse's hand, and no one shook anyone's hand more than once. My dad walked around as well (possibly shaking hands, possibly not).

At the end of the party, my dad asked everyone else at the party (including my mom) how many hands they had each shaken. To his utter amazement, every single person gave him a different answer. What number did my mom say when my dad asked her?

Tricky Twenty #4

Two old, brilliant mathematicians, Kramer and Jose, are walking down the street. Kramer asks Jose to guess the ages of his three grandchildren. Jose agrees and asks for some clues.

Kramer says the product of the three ages is 36. Jose thinks for a minute, and then says he needs another clue. Kramer says the sum of the three ages is equal to the address of the orange house across the street. Jose looks at the house's address, thinks for a minute, and then says he needs another clue. Kramer says that the younger two children occasionally wear the old clothes of the eldest child. Jose excitedly says, "Oh, now I know the ages!"

What are the ages of the three grandchildren?

Tricky Twenty #5

You sell gold coins. Ten suppliers each send you ten coins each week, each coin supposedly weighing 10 ounces. So you should be getting 100 10-ounce coins each week. You are told one of your suppliers is cheating you. He is shaving off a bit from each coin and is sending you ten 9-ounce coins each week instead of ten 10-ounce coins.

You have a scale weight (the one found in bathrooms that displays the exact weight of the object, also known as a pointer weight). What is the minimum number of times you need to use the scale to determine who is the cheating supplier?

Remember that you have a scale weight and not a balance weight.

Tricky Twenty #6

An advertising firm knows that only 10% of the people they interview are qualified to work for the firm. It also knows that it is 80% accurate in determining the true ability of a candidate (i.e., 80% of the time the firm can correctly assess that a good candidate is in fact good, and 80% of the time they can correctly assess that a bad candidate is in fact bad). Naturally, the firm hires everyone that it determines to be good. What percentage of the candidates that are hired are actually good candidates?

Tricky Twenty #7

You go to your uncle's basement. He shows you three doors and tells you that you can select a door and keep whatever is behind it. He tells you that two of the three doors have worthless goats behind them, but the other door has a new car behind it.

You initially select a door. After you select the door, your uncle opens up one of the two other doors and shows you a goat. (Regardless of what door you initially select, your uncle can always open up an unselected door that has a goat behind it.) Now your uncle gives you a choice. You can either stick with the door you initially selected, or you can switch over to the other door that has not yet been opened. (Obviously you won't want to choose the opened door, because you know it has a goat in it.)

What should you do? Should you stick with the original door, switch doors, or does it not matter?

Tricky Twenty #8

You are on a boat in the center of a circular lake. There is a robber at the edge of the lake. He runs four times faster than you row. You run faster than he runs. Your objective is to escape from the lake. This means that you must row to the edge of the lake without the robber being there to greet you (because as long as he is not waiting for you at shore, you can run outrun him to freedom). The robber will always move in an optimal direction—i.e., he will always run in the direction on the lake's edge that moves him towards you.

Can you escape?

If so, how? If not, why not?

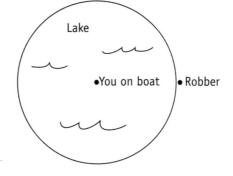

Tricky Twenty #9

You have twelve marbles. Eleven marbles are normal weight, but the twelfth marble is a slightly different weight (possibly a bit heavier, possibly a bit lighter). You have a balance scale and you are allowed to use it three times.

Can you prepare a schematic that ensures you can determine which is the odd ball and whether it is heavier or lighter than the other balls (within the allotted three weighs)?

If so, how? If not, why not?

Tricky Twenty #10

You have two ropes. After being lit on one end by a match, each rope takes exactly one hour to burn completely. The ropes do not necessarily burn at a uniform rate. The ropes do not necessarily burn at the same rate as each other. All you know is that it takes exactly one hour for each rope to burn after being lit on one end.

Can you measure 45 minutes?

If so, how? If not, why not?

Tricky Twenty #11

You have a chessboard (pictured below). You also have 32 dominoes, each of which is exactly the size of two squares on the chessboard.

It should be obvious that there are hundreds of ways to place the 32 dominoes on the chessboard so that each of the 64 squares is covered. You now take out the two opposite corner squares (marked below with arrows) and you also remove one domino. Now draw a schematic where the 31 remaining dominoes exactly cover the remaining 62 squares. If you draw such a schematic, how many unique combinations exist? If you can't draw one, prove that zero exist.

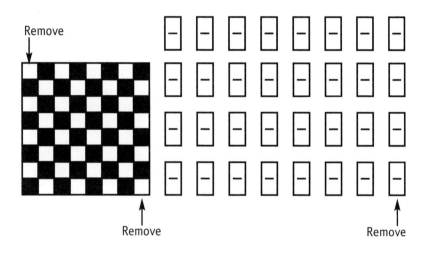

Remove

Remove

Remove

Tricky Twenty #12

Each year there is a national logic competition for high school students. This year all of the preliminary local and state tournaments have already taken place. The national final is about to occur in St. Louis, Missouri, with the three finalists—Larry, Gene, and Colin. Each of the three students is brilliant, since each has won many rigorous tournaments to qualify for this national championship final.

In St. Louis, the students will play a game to determine the champion. The following rules are explained to them: (1) they will all sit at a round table where each student can see the other two students; (2) they will close their eyes and the proctor will enter and put either a red or green hat on each of their heads; (3) they will then simultaneously open their eyes and look at each other; (4) if they see at least one red hat, they must raise their hand immediately; and (5) once they determine the color of their own hat (by observing the other two hats and whose hands are raised), they should walk out of the room and tell the proctor the answer. If a student walks out and correctly explains his logic to determine his hat color, he wins.

Now, the game begins. They all close their eyes. The proctor enters and places a red hat on each of their heads. Then they all open their eyes and they each immediately raise their hands. Then they all start doing mental calculations to determine the color of their own hat. Yet no one moves for over a minute. Then, Colin jumps up, runs out of the room, and explains why he has a red hat on. His logic is correct and he wins the competition.

How did Colin do it?

Tricky Twenty #13

Professor Diamond is busy testing his calculator to the following equation:

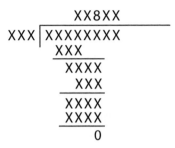

```
        XX8XX
XXX | XXXXXXXX
      XXX
      XXXX
       XXX
      XXXX
      XXXX
         0
```

His favorite pupil, Shannon, peeks over his shoulder and tells him there is only one unique solution to the equation. She also tells him that the solution is obvious and does not require a calculator. Professor Diamond disagrees and thinks many solutions exist. Is Shannon right? Is there only one solution to the equation?

Tricky Twenty #14

Time Allotted: 3 minutes.

The rectangle ABCD is inscribed inside the quadrant of the circle. What is the length of the diagonal of BD?

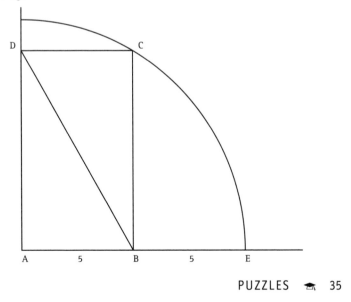

Tricky Twenty #15

1   There are five houses located next to each other.
2   The Englishman lives in the red house.
3   The Spaniard owns a dog.
4   Coffee is consumed in the green house.
5   The Ukrainian drinks tea.
6   The green house is immediately to the right of the ivory house.
7   The Old Gold smoker owns snails.
8   Kools are smoked in the yellow house.
9   Milk is consumed in the middle house.
10 The Norwegian lives in the first house (which is the left-most house).
11 The Chesterfields smoker lives next door to the man with the fox.
12 Kools are smoked in the house next to the house with the horse.
13 The Lucky Strike smoker drinks orange juice.
14 The Japanese smokes Parliaments.
15 The Norwegian lives next door to the blue house.

In each house, there is one nationality, one pet, one brand of cigarettes smoked, and one liquid drink. Who drinks water? And who owns the zebra?

Tricky Twenty #16

You are climbing up a set of steps. You can climb either one or two steps at a time. How many different ways can you take to get to the ninth step? How about the sixteenth step? How about the nth step?

For example, if there were four steps, there would be a total of five ways, namely: (1) 2-2, (2) 2-1-1, (3) 1-1-2, (4) 1-2-1, and (5) 1-1-1-1.

Tricky Twenty #17

Warren makes three six-sided dice. He used each number from 1 to 18 once on the three dice. He makes a red die (7, 4, 18, 3, 17, 8), a white die (5, 13, 10, 9, 14, 6), and a blue die (15, 1, 11, 16, 2, 12). Each die has the same sum of 57.

Warren then bets Bill $100 that he can roll a higher number than Bill. They flip a coin to determine who selects the first die, and the coin flip indicates that Bill selects his die first. So Bill studies the three dice, selects one, and then Warren intelligently selects one of the two remaining dice. They then both simultaneously roll the dice, and whoever rolls a higher number wins the $100. Assuming that both Warren and Bill are intelligent (i.e., pick the most strategic die available), what is the probability that Bill wins the bet?

Tricky Twenty #18

Ben and Hillary perform a magic trick. With a standard deck of cards, they ask a bystander to select five cards. These five cards are given only to Ben. He looks at the five cards, selects a card, orders the remaining four cards in any order he wants, and then hands these four cards to Hillary. She then names the card that remains in Ben's hands.

How is this magic trick done?

The deck that is used has a symmetrical design, so there is no distinction between handing a card and handing a card after turning it around. The cards must all be passed face down to Hillary. In other words, the only degree of freedom that Ben has is that he can select which card to keep and he can choose how to order the other four cards before handing them to Hillary.

Tricky Twenty #19

You are forced to marry one of three sisters. One always tells the truth, one always lies, and the other does equal amounts of both (i.e. half of the time she tells the truth, half of the time she lies). However, the one that tells half truth and half lies is also a werewolf (i.e. she turns into a monster at night). You are allowed to ask just one yes-no question to one of the three sisters, but you don't know who is who (i.e. you don't know which one tells the truth, which one lies, and which one is the werewolf). You are happy to marry either the truth-teller or the liar, since both are fully human. You do not want to marry the werewolf sister, because she will kill you at night when she turns into a monster.

The three sisters are standing next to each other. Can you approach one sister and ask a question (that must be answered with a simple yes or no) that will guarantee you do not select the werewolf as the bride?

If so, how? If not, why not?

Tricky Twenty #20

I once made a mathematical conjecture. Is it true?

If so, why? If not, why not?

Srinivas' conjecture:
Using exactly four 4s and the operations $+$, $-$, $\times$, $/$, $*$, $\sqrt{\ }$ (square root), . (decimal point), and ! (factorial), you can derive at least 95 of the integers from 1 to 100.

Here are two examples of using exactly four 4s:

$26 = 4! + \sqrt{4} \times (.4/.4)$
$28 = (4!/ \sqrt{4})/.4 - \sqrt{4}$

Part 2

Solutions

Brain Teaser #1

Answer:

        26 = Letters of the Alphabet
         7 = Wonders of the Ancient World
      1001 = Arabian Nights
        12 = Signs of the Zodiac
        54 = Cards in a Deck (with the Jokers)
         9 = Planets in the Solar System
        88 = Piano Keys
        13 = Stripes on the American Flag
        18 = Holes on a Golf Course
        32 = Degrees Fahrenheit at which Water Freezes
         8 = Sides on a Stop Sign
         3 = Blind Mice (See How They Run)
        90 = Degrees in a Right Angle
        24 = Hours in a Day
        57 = Heinz Varieties
        11 = Players on a Football Team
      1000 = Words that a Picture is Worth
        29 = Days in February in a Leap Year
       200 = Dollars for Passing Go in Monopoly
         5 = Digits in a Zip Code

The best way to solve this puzzle is to think long and hard.

This test gauges your mental flexibility. In the few years since it was developed, supposedly very few people have arrived at even half of the correct answers on a first try. There are stories, however, of people getting the right answers long after putting the test aside, particularly when their minds weren't even thinking at all about the riddle.

I have received this puzzle several times, most recently from Rachel Davis, who was a colleague of mine at Goldman Sachs. She currently works at an advertising firm in New York City.

Brain Teaser #2

Answer: $1.19.

There are three possible ways to have $1.19.
The first is: three quarters, four dimes, and four pennies.
The second is: one quarter, nine dimes, and four pennies.
The third is: one half-dollar, one quarter, four dimes, and four pennies.

Veerendra Prasad, a childhood friend, asked me this riddle a few years ago. He is currently a filmmaker in Hollywood.

Brain Teaser #3

Answer: 31 lockers.

I have witnessed many friends try to write computer code to solve this riddle. A few have succeeded, but most fail. Unfortunately for me, I don't remember too much from the computer classes that I took in college.

For any locker X, the number of times that locker is opened or closed is equal to the number of factors that X has. For example, locker 28 will be opened or closed a total of six times. In particular, students 1, 2, 4, 7, 14, and 28 (which are the six factors of 28) will all change the position of the door of locker 28.

All 1000 lockers are initially open. So all lockers that are changed an even number of times will end up open, because the first person closes it, the second opens it, the third closes it, the fourth opens it, etc. Likewise, all lockers that are changed an odd number of times will end up closed. So now the problem boils down to finding all of the numbers between 1 and 1000 that have an odd number of factors.

A random sampling of numbers (such as 6, 17, 24, and 35) shows that most numbers seem to have an even number of factors. This is because it seems easy to pair up factors. I define pair up as matching factors that multiply to give the original number. For example, for the number 24, there are a total of eight factors. They can be paired as: 1–24, 2–12, 3–9, and 4–6. So we have to find numbers where all of the factors can't be paired up.

With a little thought, it should be evident that perfect squares (such as 1, 4, 9, and 16) all have an odd number of factors. Take 36 for example. The 1 pairs up with the 36, the 2 pairs up with the 18, the 3 pairs up with the 12, the 4 pairs up with the 9, but the 6 is alone since it really pairs up with itself. Hence, the number 36 (like all other perfect squares) has an odd number of factors. With a calculator, it is easy to realize there are 31 perfect squares between 1 and 1000. Hence, the 31 lockers that end up closed are: 1, 4, 9, 16, 25, 36, 49, 64, 81, 100, 121, 144, 169, 196, 225, 256, 289, 324, 361, 400, 441, 529, 576, 625, 676, 729, 784, 841, 900, and 961.

Gorav Jindal asked me this riddle during a game of bridge. I did solve the puzzle, but I got annihilated in the card game. Gorav is a lawyer in Washington, D.C. at Dechert & Company.

Brain Teaser #4

Part 1 answer: Yes, it is possible to make five squares with twelve toothpicks.

Part 2 answer: Yes, it is possible to make four equilateral triangles with six toothpicks.

In Part 1, the insight is to realize the five squares don't necessarily have to be the same size. In fact, the riddle can only be solved if the squares are different sizes. The following diagram shows twelve toothpicks in the shape of four small squares and one large square:

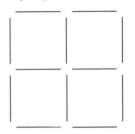

This riddle was asked as an extra-credit problem on my middle school geometry class final exam.

In Part 2, the ingenuity is to think in three dimensions. If you take six toothpicks and form a pyramid (like those famous ones in Egypt), you will create an object that has four sides, all of which are equilateral triangles. Here is a diagram:

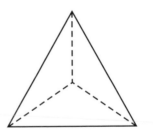

This type of question is frequently asked in the geometry portion of junior high school math competitions. The test creators are trying to force the contestants to "think outside the two-dimensional box."

Brain Teaser #5

Answer: March 30.

The insight is to work backward. On March 31, the pond is 100% filled. Therefore, on March 30, the pond must be 50% filled (this is the only way the pond can be 100% filled on March 31). So on March 29, the pond is only 25% filled (this is the only way the pond can be 50% filled on March 30). Hence, March 30 is the first day the pond is at least 30% covered by lily flowers.

My three MathCounts teammates and I were asked a simpler version of this riddle in eighth grade at the Michigan State finals. MathCounts is a national math competition for junior high school students consisting of both team and individual events. Our team needed three of the four members to independently answer the question correctly within two minutes to win the state title. Only two of us answered it correctly and consequently we ended up with a disappointing third-place finish (and missed a chance to go to the national finals).

Brain Teaser #6

Answer: The water level would fall.

Initially when the lead anchor is on the boat, the mass of water that is displaced upward is equal to the mass of the lead anchor. This is a lot of water since the lead anchor is heavy. When the lead anchor is dropped into the water, the volume of water displaced upward is equal to the volume of the lead anchor. The lead anchor is denser than water, so the amount of water equal to the mass of the lead anchor is greater than the amount of water equal to the volume of the lead anchor. Thus, when the lead anchor is dropped into the lake, there is less water that is being pushed upward, and hence the water level of the lake falls.

My good friend Paul Kwan, who now works at Morgan Stanley in Menlo Park, California, asked me this riddle. He was asked this question in his senior year at Stanford during a high-technology–firm interview.

Brain Teaser #7

Answer: Four socks.

In the first three selections, you could, in the worst case, pull out a green sock, a yellow sock, and a red sock. However, with your fourth selection, you will definitely pick a color that has already been picked, and hence you will surely have a matching pair of socks.

My mom asked me this question many years ago. Even though it is a straightforward, simple riddle, many people often come up with answers of seven, nine, and fifteen.

Brain Teaser #8

Answer: 7.5°.

When the time is 3:15, the minute hand is exactly on the 3. The hour hand, however, is ¼ of the way between the 3 and the 4, since 3:15 is ¼ of the way between 3:00 and 4:00. There are 360° in a circle. Since there are twelve markers on a clock, there are 30° between each pair of hour markers. Given that the hour and minute hands are separated by ¼ of the distance between two adjacent hour markers, they are separated by ¼ of 30°, which is 7.5°.

This is a popular question at investment banking interviews. This is baffling to me, because I don't think that the skill needed to solve this riddle is necessary to be a good investment banker. Sadly, many candidates try to impress the interviewer with brain speed and give an answer of 0°—only later realizing that their logic is flawed.

Brain Teaser #9

Answer: 488.

Most people initially say 600, since there are 100 small cubes visible on each of the six sides. This logic is wrong, since the cubes on the edges and corners of the big cube should not be double- or triple-counted. It is possible to accurately visualize each edge and corner and consequently solve the riddle by counting the visible 488 cubes.

In my opinion, there exists a more simple and elegant solution. The inside of the bigger cube (the section not visible at all to the eye) is just an $8 \times 8 \times 8$ cube. This means there are 512 smaller cubes (which is equal to 8^3) that aren't visible. If 512 of the 1000 smaller cubes are not visible, then 488 of the smaller cubes must be visible.

This type of question has been asked to me a few times in interviews at both consulting firms and investment banks. Fortunately for me, my dad asked me this riddle many years ago before I started interviewing.

Brain Teaser #10

Part 1 answer: *Sovereignty.*

Part 2 answer: *Facetiously.*

Part 3 answer: *Bookkeeper.*

Anuragh Mehta, a college classmate, asked me Part 1 when we were in school. He is currently at Harvard Law School. He is a grammar fiend and is confident that *sovereignty* is the only word that fits this requirement. To date, I have asked many people this question and no one has been able to come up with a word other than *sovereignty*.

David Rice, a high school friend, asked me Part 2. He works for Intel in Phoenix, Arizona. To my surprise, many people have solved this riddle. Most people eventually realize that the letters *iou* are grouped together, since this is a common letter sequence in the English language. They also correctly figure out that the word ends in the letter *y*. Given these two correct deductions (and a lot of spare time), it is possible to solve for the word *facetiously*.

Bill Hoffman asked me Part 3. He is an author from Diamondhead, Mississippi. This riddle is very tricky because there are many words with two consecutive double letters or three non-consecutive double letters, but *bookkeeper* is the only word that has three consecutive double letters.

Brain Teaser #11

Answer: Yes, you can do it.

The three light bulbs are initially off, and the switches are in the off position. You flip on two of the switches. You wait for a long time. Then, you switch off one of the two switches that you had earlier flipped on. Now, you enter the room. One light bulb will be on, and you will know that light is connected to the switch that is still in the on position. The other two light bulbs are off. You walk over and touch them. One of them will still be hot from being on for a long period of time, and you will know that light is connected to the switch you turned on and later turned off. The other light is connected to the switch you never touched.

Josh Uy asked me this puzzle on a white-water rafting trip. Josh is currently at Michigan Medical School.

Brain Teaser #12

Answer: It never existed.

Most people try to build a total of $30 in a similar fashion to what was done in the riddle. In particular, if the three guests each paid $9, that gives a sum of $27. Then adding the clerk's $2 gives a total of $29, which is $1 short of the original $30 that was paid. However, this logic is wrong.

In the end, the three guests paid a total of $27. Of that $27 dollars, $25 is with the cashier and $2 is with the clerk. That's it. Nothing more. (Another way to think of it is that there is originally $30 paid. Of that original $30, the cashier keeps $25, the guests get $3 back, and the clerk steals $2.)

This riddle has circulated for years. Most recently, Sapna Vyas, a doctoral candidate at Michigan State University, asked me this riddle.

Brain Teaser #13

Answer: Six Fs.

There are no gimmicks—there are six Fs in the sentence. I counted two Fs when this question was first asked to me. Even after someone explicitly told me that there were six Fs, I still could only count three Fs on my second try.

In fact, more than 75% of the people that I sampled this question to counted no more than four Fs. This puzzle shows that it is easy to see something, yet not process the information properly because we try to work at high speeds. Hence, the riddle reveals that focus and concentration are as important as pure brains and raw speed.

Jugdeep Bal, a good friend, sent me this riddle when he was working at First USA Bank in Philadelphia, Pennsylvania.

Brain Teaser #14

Answer: They are equally diluted—the jar has as much orange juice as the mug has apple juice.

The most direct solution involves significant algebra (calculating the ratios of each container after each liquid transfer). But this is a tedious solution, with a high probability of computational error.

The elegant solution is to realize that after both transfers, there are still 10 liters of liquid in the jar and 10 liters in the mug. Assume that there are x units of orange juice in the jar. That means that there are $10 - x$ units of apple juice in the jar. Furthermore, since there must be a total of 10 liters of apple juice between the two containers, there must be x units of apple juice in the mug. And since there are 10 total liters in the mug, there must be $10 - x$ units of orange juice still in the mug.

So there is the same amount of apple juice in the mug as orange juice in the jar (and the same amount of apple juice in the jar as orange juice in the mug).

I was asked this puzzle in a final-round hedge fund interview. The version I was asked was more difficult because the interviewer had a total of six liquid transfers (i.e., a liter from the jar to the mug, then a liter from the mug to the jar, then a liter from the jar to the mug, etc.). However, the underlying logic is the same.

After I solved the riddle, I asked the interviewer his own puzzle with an additional twist. I asked him if it were possible (without dumping all of the liquid into one vessel) to keep transporting 1 liter back and forth such that both containers have the same percentage of apple juice in them. He got flustered and couldn't answer the puzzle. The answer is no. This is because whenever liquid is moved from a higher concentration container to a lower concentration container, the initial container will still have the higher concentration (and likewise the opposite is true when liquid is moved from a lower concentration container to a higher concentration container). So, without mixing all of the liquid in one container, it is impossible to equalize the concentrations of both containers.

Brain Teaser #15

Answer: The minimum number of matches is 206. The maximum number of matches is also 206.

At first glance, it is very surprising that the minimum and maximum number of matches are the same. However, regardless of how the brackets are created, there will always be a total of 206 matches.

There are many ways to set up a tournament bracket. Here are two examples. First, you could assign a number to each person. Then, you could have #207 play #206. The winner of that match would play #205. Then, the winner of that match would play #204, etc. This is similar to many bowling tournaments, where the #1 seed is guaranteed of playing in the finals since he or she waits until everyone else plays in the ladder until only one other participant remains. A second way to arrange the brackets is to have 103 first-round matches (with a single person having a bye). Then, with the 103 first-round winners and with the one bye, you have a total of 52 second-round matches. Then, with the 52 second-round winners, you have a total of 27 third-round matches. You keep doing this and insert byes when necessary. Both of these examples have very different bracket schedules and you can imagine that there are hundreds of more ways to arrange the brackets.

However, regardless of how you schedule the games and the byes, there is no way to change the total number of games played. It will always be 206. This is easy to prove. At the end of the tournament, there will be 206 people who have lost a single match and one champion (who never lost). We know that each match played leads to one loser. Hence, if there are a total of 206 losers in the end, there must have been 206 matches played (since each match produces a unique loser).

This logic can be broadly applied. I was once at a restaurant watching the NCAA college basketball tournament. For those of you who aren't college basketball fans (shame on you), the NCAA tournament starts out with 64 teams and has a standard bracket where in each sequential round there are 32, 16, 8, 4, 2, and 1 team(s) remaining (with that last team remaining being the college champion). A friend of mine claimed he was going to watch every single game. I quickly replied that watching 63 games in 19 days seemed overambitious. The other dinner guests were amazed that I was able to calculate the number of tournament games so quickly.

Brain Teaser #16

Part 1 answer: Carson City, Nevada
Jefferson City, Missouri
Oklahoma City, Oklahoma
Salt Lake City, Utah

Part 2 answer: Dover, Delaware
Honolulu, Hawaii
Indianapolis, Indiana
Oklahoma City, Oklahoma

Part 1 was asked to a friend of mine at her interview with Intel. She got three of the four answers. (She missed Jefferson City, Missouri.) But she still got the job offer. I was surprised that a high-technology firm would ask such a question, but I presume it underscores the importance of general knowledge for any type of job.

Part 2 was asked to me at a trading interview. I answered it and immediately asked the interviewer Part 1, which he failed to solve. Again, this seems like an irrelevant question for a trader to know, but it reiterates the importance of general knowledge in today's workplace.

Brain Teaser #17

Answer: You need only two uses of the balance scale.

Label the marbles 1 through 9. On the first use, weigh marbles 1, 2, and 3 versus 4, 5, and 6. If one side moves upward, you know that side contains the lighter marble. If they balance, you know the lighter marble is among 7, 8, and 9. Hence, after one weigh, you have narrowed the lighter marble down to one group of three marbles. Of these three marbles, weigh any one against another. If one side moves upward, that side contains the light marble. Otherwise, the lighter marble is the one you did not weigh (of the three marbles). Hence, with just two uses of the balance scale, you can ensure that the lighter marble can be found.

This question is popular at law firm and investment-banking interviews. Sadly most people give an answer of three weighs (because they wrongly assume that the first weigh has four marbles weighed against four other marbles). The insight here is to realize that you not only get valuable information when the two sides are uneven, but you also get equally important information when the two sides balance.

Many interviewers like this question because they think it is the pinnacle of tricky balance-scale riddles. They are very mistaken. If you are ever asked this riddle, quickly answer it, and then pose the interviewer a more difficult balance-scale or bathroom-scale riddle (such riddles are still to come).

Brain Teaser #18

Answer: 27,499,951.

There are several ways to solve this puzzle. The most obvious is via brute force, but this will take much longer than the allotted 5 minutes. Additionally, a brute-force methodology has a high probability of computational error.

The insight here is to group the numbers into pairs, thereby simplifying the problem. More specifically, group the numbers in the following manner: (1–999,999), (2–999,998), (3–999,997), ..., (499,998–500,002), and (499,999–500,001). This grouping excludes 500,000 and 1,000,000.

Each pair of numbers has a digital sum of 55. There are 499,999 pairs. So the sum of all the digits in the paired numbers is simply $55 \times 499,999 =$ 27,499,945. However, we must add the digit values in the two excluded numbers, namely 500,000 and 1,000,000. We therefore add a value of 6 to our previous sum to incorporate these two unpaired numbers. This gives us a final sum of 27,499,951.

Brain Teaser #19

Answer: It is impossible to do.

Many people believe that the answer is 90 mph or 120 mph. But both of these answers are wrong.

Suppose that Chicago and Toledo are 120 miles apart. (The actual number of miles is irrelevant since any number would lead to the same conclusion—120 miles is used only for simplicity in calculations.) It would take 4 hours to travel from Chicago to Toledo, since you traveled at 30 mph. The whole trip (both to and from) is 240 miles, so to average 60 mph on the full trip your total travel time needs to be 4 hours. However, the first leg of the trip already exhausted 4 hours. Thus, unless you can get from Toledo to Chicago in no time, it is impossible to do. If you had substituted x for 120 miles, you would have arrived at the same conclusion—namely, 60 mph is unachievable.

I was asked this puzzle at a derivatives trading interview. Traders love to test corner solutions and this puzzle effectively tests an extreme corner situation. This is because if you had traveled any faster than 30 mph on the first leg or if your overall desired speed was any less than 60 mph, it would be possible to drive at some speed on the second leg to achieve your desired overall speed. However, the two variables (30 mph on first leg, 60 mph overall speed) create an unsolvable corner situation.

Brain Teaser #20

Answer: Yes, you can ask a question that assures that you walk away to freedom.

The difficulty is that you don't know to whom (the truth-teller or the liar) you are asking your question. So a question such as, "Which door leads to freedom?" is useless because the truth-teller will point to one door (the freedom door) and the liar will point to the other door (the lions door). Since you don't know whom you are asking, you have no idea whether or not to go through the suggested door.

You have to devise a question that gives the same answer regardless of whom you are asking (since you don't know which guard is which). You should ask, "If I were to ask the other guard which door leads to freedom, what would he say?"

This question will allow you to escape from jail. Here's why. Suppose you ask the truth-teller. He knows the other guard will lie and point to the wrong door. Since he is a truth-teller, he will answer honestly and point to the wrong door (since this is what the other guard would have said). Now, suppose you had asked the liar. He knows the other guard will tell the truth and point to the right door. Since he is a liar, he will point to the wrong door (since this is not what the other guard would have said).

Hence, regardless of whom you ask the question, "If I were to ask the other guard which door leads to freedom, what would he say?" you will always get the same answer, which is the lions door. So you should just exit through the other door (the one the guard does not point to), since you know that is the door toward freedom.

This puzzle has many variations. A friend of mine solved the puzzle using what she calls pseudo-math. She tried to apply the basic principle that $1 \times -1 = -1 \times 1 = -1$. She considered the truth-teller to be 1 and the liar to be -1, so she needed to devise a question that included both of them. She needed a question that had the guard describe the other guard (this effectively represents multiplication), so she could arrive at an answer of -1 (which also represents the wrong door). With this clever insight, she was able to quickly figure out the right question to ask.

My dad's friend asked me this puzzle at a dinner party.

Brain Teaser #21

Answer: Yes, very easily in fact.

The tractor is a decoy. If the plot of land is 1 mile × 1 mile, then the diagonal of the land is approximately 1.41 mile (using the Pythagorean theorem). Hence, a runway of 1.25 miles could easily fit on your land as long as it runs somewhat along the diagonal of the land.

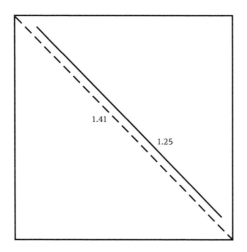

This question tests the ability to discern useless information. It is often asked in interviews by consulting firms. I believe this is because a consulting project can often take months to finish, and during a project life there will be many pieces of research and information that are utterly useless. Hence, consultants need to be especially good at evaluating vast amounts of information and quickly gauging which of it is important.

Brain Teaser #22

Answer: 3 meters.

The common solution to this puzzle uses a lot of math. The ball travels 1 meter before it first hits the ground. Then, it travels another 1 meter before hitting the ground again (0.5 meter up, 0.5 meter down). Then, it travels 0.5 meter before hitting the ground again (0.25 meter up, 0.25 meter down). Then it travels 0.25 meter before hitting the ground again. The following equation calculates the total distance the ball travels:

$$
\begin{aligned}
\text{Total distance} &= 1 + 1 + \tfrac{1}{2} + \tfrac{1}{4} + \tfrac{1}{8} + \tfrac{1}{16} + \ldots \\
&= 2 + \tfrac{1}{2} + \tfrac{1}{4} + \tfrac{1}{8} + \tfrac{1}{16} + \ldots \\
&= 2 + \textstyle\sum (\tfrac{1}{2})^{\wedge}n, \text{ where } n \text{ is all integers from 1 to infinity} \\
&= 2 + [\text{first term}/(1 - \text{term factor})] \\
&= 2 + [(\tfrac{1}{2})/(1 - \tfrac{1}{2})] \\
&= 2 + [(\tfrac{1}{2})/(\tfrac{1}{2})] \\
&= 2 + 1 \\
&= 3
\end{aligned}
$$

The first line is the sum of all distances traveled between touches of the ground (the first term is the distance until the ball first hits the ground). From geometry, we remember the sum for an infinite series [first term/ (1−term factor)], which is shown in the fourth line. Since the term factor is $\tfrac{1}{2}$ (this is the ratio of each successive term), we can use simple arithmetic to fully solve for the answer.

A more back-of-the-envelope calculation—which is how I like to solve these types of puzzles—is to take out a calculator and start adding terms. By just adding the first 6 terms, you have a sum of 2.9375. With each successive term, it becomes clear that the sum is converging toward 3.

This second solution seems cheap, but I assure you the skill involved to think of it is very useful. This skill is the ability to find the bulk of value in a large (or even infinite) set of numbers by focusing on a few key numbers. For example, as a Goldman Sachs analyst, I often had to value a company. The value of a company is generally defined as the sum of all future cash flows (because as an owner of a company you are legally entitled to all the future cash flows). Assuming that the company will last forever (which is reasonable for McDonald's, Ford, Microsoft, etc.), there will be an infinite number of annual cash flows. However, in most cases, the sum of the first ten to twelve cash flows gives a good approximation of the exact value of the company (due to the time value of money). Thus, this so-called cheap skill is useful because instead of trying to sum up an infinite number of cash flows, a simple sum of the first dozen or so cash flows gives a useful approximation of value.

This is a popular investment banking and consulting puzzle. My friend Ketan Sanghvi was asked this question at an interview for Manhattan Associates in Greenwich, Connecticut.

Brain Teaser #23

Answer: You probably have a gray elephant from Denmark.

Over 90% of my sample population for this puzzle came up with this answer. The mathematics forces the final number always to be 4, thereby forcing the initial letter to be *D*. There are several countries that start with *D*, including Denmark, Dubai, Dominican Republic, and Djibouti. However, most people settle on Denmark. Likewise, there are several animals that start with *E*, including elephant, eel, and elk. However, most people settle on *elephant*.

This puzzle has circulated for several years.

Brain Teaser #24

Answer: The minimum percentage that could have lost all four body parts is 10%.

For explanation's sake, assume that there are 100 men (any number arrives at the same conclusion; 100 is selected for ease of calculation). There are a total of 310 injuries (70 + 75 + 80 + 85). In the most extreme scenario, in which the injuries are most evenly distributed, a total of 310 injuries means that each soldier still has (at least) three injuries. In fact, it should be obvious that ten soldiers must have all four injuries (otherwise with no one having all four injuries, the maximum number of injuries is 300). Hence, the minimum percentage of people that have all four injuries is 10%.

On a side note, if the question had asked what is the maximum percentage of the troops that lost all four body parts, the answer would have been 70%. This is when everyone who lost an arm (70% of the people) also had injuries to a leg, an ear, and an eye. It is not 77.5%, which is 310/4, since the arm constraint is the most limiting constraint for the maximum scenario.

Lewis Carroll, the author of Alice in Wonderland, *created this riddle. He was a fanatic of brain teasers, and is credited with creating some of today's most difficult puzzles. This puzzle was supposedly his favorite.*

Brain Teaser #25

Part 1 answer: 50%.

Part 2 answer: ⅓ (approximately 33%).

Part 1 is very basic. It should be evident that the younger child's sex is independent of the older child's sex. Since each child has an equal chance of being a boy or girl, the younger child has a 50% probability of being a boy.

Part 2 is a completely different riddle. It highlights the importance of wording. Without any restrictions, there are four equally likely outcomes for the distribution of the sexes. Specifically, they are:

Scenario #	Older Child	Younger Child
1	Boy	Boy
2	Boy	Girl
3	Girl	Boy
4	Girl	Girl

However, we do know that (at least) one child is a boy (we are unsure whether it is the older or the younger). Hence, we can eliminate the last scenario (#4). Now, there are three equally likely scenarios. In only one of these remaining scenarios is the second child also a boy. Thus, the answer is ⅓.

Both parts of this question were on a statistics exam that I took at Stanford. Most students wrongly answered 50% for both parts (by reasoning that each child is independent of the other child). These students failed to understand the logic of the second question. The second question effectively is a conditional probability puzzle—it asks what is the probability of having two boys, given at least one boy.

The logic may still be confusing. Another way to understand the answer is to do an empirical test. List all of the families that you know with two children. Then circle all of those that have at least one boy. These circled families represent the population in the second riddle, since there is a prerequisite of having one boy. Of this circled set, count the percentage that have a second boy as well. With a large enough sample size, you should approach an answer of ⅓.

Brain Teaser #26

Answer: Yes. It is possible to bowl a 99 having 8 strikes and no gutter balls.

A handful of solutions exist. Here is one example:

Frame:	1	2	3	4	5	6	7	8	9	10
Score:	10	10	1-0	10	1-0	10	1-0	10	1-0	10 10 10
Cumulative Score:	21	32	33	44	45	56	57	68	69	99

The above scorecard gives a final score of 99.

The insight is a bit tricky, but any recreational bowler should be able to figure it out. A gutter ball is exactly what its name suggests—a ball that enters the gutter (there is one on each side of a bowling lane). In frames 3, 5, 7, and 9, you could bowl your first ball such that it knocks down either pin #7 or pin #10 (which are the two outside pins in the last row). Then, on your second ball, you could bowl in the exact same location of the first ball such that the ball rolls down the lane into the back alley without ever entering the gutter. This would give you a score of 0, but you would not have rolled a gutter ball.

Let me clarify this concept. Think of a situation where two pins remain after the first bowl and the two pins are on opposite sides of each other. If you were to bowl right between the pins such that neither pin falls down, you would not consider this a gutter ball (in fact, a nickname for such a bowl is field goal). It should be clear that it is very possible to bowl a 0 without it being a gutter ball. I admit that the field goal type 0 scores occur more often than the situation I described above, but nonetheless both are still non–gutter-ball 0 scores.

Sarat Ramayya, a consultant at Manhattan Associates in Atlanta, Georgia, asked me this riddle. He was originally asked this riddle on a plane. My friend Satya Patel, an associate at GeoCapital Partners in Fort Lee, New Jersey, was the captain of his high school bowling team, and he solved the riddle within minutes.

Brain Teaser #27

Answer: No. It is impossible to construct two drives such that you are never at the exact same location at the exact same time on the two consecutive Sundays.

Most people vehemently argue that it is possible to construct a drive that satisfies the necessary conditions. They suggest that on the first leg of the trip you drive really, really slowly for 11 hours 59 minutes and then zoom in the last minute (i.e., spend most of the trip near Atlanta but in the last minute cover most of the distance). They continue their argument by saying that on the return trip, you again drive really, really slowly for 11 hours 59 minutes and then zoom in the last minute (i.e., spend most of the trip near Detroit but in the last minute cover most of the distance). They claim this situation satisfies the necessary conditions in the riddle because in the first trip all of the 12 hours are effectively near Atlanta and on the return trip all of the time is effectively near Detroit. As convincing as the argument seems, it is wrong.

This riddle can be solved using calculus (continuity theorems), but there is a more elegant solution. Just superimpose the two drives. Imagine that it is 8 AM right now and both drives are starting—your initial drive from Atlanta and your return drive from Detroit. This is what effectively happens, though in reality the drives are exactly one week apart. Now, let a clock run for 12 hours. At the end of the 12 hours, both drives must finish. Regardless of the speed of the two drives, there is a point where the two cars cross each other's paths. The two drives are going in opposite directions on the same path so at some point they must cross each other. (In the above example, the crossing point occurs in the last minute of the trip.) Therefore, it is impossible to construct a scenario such that you are not at the same location at the same time on the two separate Sundays.

This riddle is almost impossible to solve without creating a superimposition of the two drives; hence, it tests visual and spatial thinking skills. The ability to superimpose situations and think spatially is very useful in many applications.

Vinod Prasad, who now works at Broadcom in San Jose, California, asked me this puzzle. He was asked a similar riddle on an engineering exam in graduate school (though he was required to provide a calculus-based solution).

Brain Teaser #28

Answer: If you were willing to pay your expected value, you would be willing to pay infinity dollars (i.e., you would pay any amount of money to play the game).

Wow, what an unsatisfying answer. In my opinion, this unsatisfying answer is what makes this puzzle so interesting. In one-half of the times you play, you end up with only $1 in winnings (since one-half of the games end on the first flip). In another one-quarter of the times you play, you end up with only $2 (this is when you first flip a head followed immediately by a tail). Thus, in three-quarters of the games, you will receive at most $2 in winnings. Intuitively, you would suspect that you do not want to pay more than $2, if that, to play this game.

However, most people agree that expected value is the fair amount to pay to play. So, let's solve for the expected value:

Expected winnings = Sum of [probability of each occurrence $\times$ its associated payoff]

$$= (1/2 \times 1) + (1/4 \times 2) + (1/8 \times 4) + (1/16 \times 8) + (1/32 \times 16) + \ldots$$
$$= 1/2 + 1/2 + 1/2 + 1/2 + 1/2 + \ldots$$
$$= \text{Infinity}$$

The first line of the equation is definition. The second line is the sum of the probability of each occurrence multiplied by its associated payoff. The probability of each occurrence is equal to $1/2 \char`^ t$, where t is the number of total flips. This is most easily understood by example. The probability of getting HHHHHT (and winning $16) is equal to $1/2 \times 1/2 \times 1/2 \times 1/2 \times 1/2 \times 1/2 = 1/64$. This is because the probability of each of the six coin flips being the desired head or tail is $1/2$. Simple arithmetic takes us from the second line to our final answer of infinity. Hence, in theory you should be willing to pay any amount of money to play. However, this answer is quite unintuitive.

I was asked this in a Goldman Sachs trading interview. After solving it, the interviewer asked me in reality what I would pay to play. I said between $4 and $6. We then had a discussion on why I said that amount. This is a terrific interview question because not only is it difficult to answer correctly, but once the answer is established, it is possible to have an engaging conversation about what one would pay in reality and why. This follow-up discussion is very interesting because it challenges one to think about how much risk one is willing to take for this eccentric reward profile.

Brain Teaser #29

Answer: 16.

The most common answer is eight, because it flows with the question. However, if four hens can lay four eggs in four minutes, that means it takes a single hen four minutes to lay a single egg. So if you have eight hens, each being able to lay an egg in four minutes, that means that they can each lay two eggs in eight minutes, which gives a total of sixteen eggs.

A friend of mine was asked this at a final-round venture capital interview. He didn't get the answer and didn't get the job offer.

Brain Teaser #30

Answer: 23 people.

This is an eye-popping solution because 23 people seems like such a small number. This means that in every elementary, high school, and college class of at least 23 students, there is a better than 50% probability that at least two people share the same birthday. Or in any sports stadium with a row of at least 23 fans, there is more than a 50% chance that there is a duplicate birthday. Can this be?

Yes. Here's why. Assume the first person has his birthday on day A. Now, the probability that the second person has his birthday on another day, say day B, is 364/365. The probability that the third person has his birthday on some other day besides A or B, let's say day C, is 363/365. The probability that the fourth person has his birthday on some other day besides A, B, or C, let's say day D, is 362/365, etc. This above condition of separate birthdays is the opposite of what we are looking for. Remember, we are looking for a situation in which multiple birthdays fall on the same day. But the easiest way to solve this riddle is to first solve for the probability that all of the birthdays are on different days. We know that (1−that probability) is equal to the probability of identical birthdays.

More formally, we are looking for the smallest n such that:

$$\tfrac{1}{2} > (364/365) \times (363/365) \times (362/365) \times \ldots \times ((366 - n)/365)$$

The rational for using $(366-n)$ is best explained by example. For instance, in the case of two people we want to use 364 (which is $366-2$) for the last individual numerator. Likewise, for four people, we want to use 362 (which is $366-4$) for the last numerator. From elementary math, we remember that if we want to find the probabilities of different, independent events, we should multiply the probabilities. In our situation, the birthday of each person is an independent event.

With a calculator, it is easy to solve that n = 23 (you keep multiplying terms until the product falls under $\tfrac{1}{2}$). This means that when there are 23 people in a group, there is less than a 50% probability that everyone has different birthdays. In order words, this also means that there is a greater than 50% probability that there are duplicate birthdays.

Over the years, I have seen many solutions to this riddle, but I still believe that the above solution is the easiest to understand.

This puzzle was asked as an extra-credit question on a statistics exam at Stanford. Most students just guessed 183 (which is the smallest number that is greater than one-half of 365). However, as we saw the real answer of 23 is much lower. This is a situation in which intuition leads to a completely wrong solution.

Brain Teaser #31

Answer: Your maximum probability of survival is 14/19 (which is approximately 73.7%).

The optimal strategy is to put one white ball in the first box and place the remaining 19 balls in the other box. The probability of selecting each box is 50%, so whenever the first box is chosen (which is 50% of the time), you survive. Whenever the second box is chosen (also 50% of the time), your probability of survival is 9 out of 19 (which is approximately 47.4%). From algebra, we remember that:

Probability of survival = (probability of selecting first box × probability of survival if first box is chosen) + (probability of selecting second box × probability of survival if second box is chosen)
$$= (\text{\textonehalf} \times 1) + (\text{\textonehalf} \times 9/19)$$
$$= 0.500 + 0.237$$
$$= 0.737$$
$$= 73.7\%$$

Hence, the maximum probability of survival is approximately 73.7%.

I was asked this during a trading interview at Goldman Sachs in 1998. As previously mentioned, traders frequently ask questions that have corner solutions. In this question, the most extreme (corner) situation is to place all 20 balls in one box, but that only gives you a 50% chance of survival. However, the next most extreme (corner) situation is to have 19 balls in one box.

Most people initially try solving this riddle by using a more typical middle solution. In other words, they assume that 10 balls should be put in each box. However, if 10 balls are put in each box, the probability of survival will always be 50%, regardless of the composition of white and black balls in each box. This is intuitive because as one box has more white balls (and a greater survival probability), the other box will have correspondingly more black balls (and a greater death probability). These influences exactly counter each other and the overall survival probability will remain 50%. Hence, solutions such as: (1) 5 white, 5 black in Box 1 and 5 white, 5 black in Box 2, (2) 7 white, 3 black in Box 1 and 3 white, 7 black in Box 2, or (3) 10 white, 0 black in Box 1 and 0 white, 10 black in Box 2, all lead to a survival probability of 50%.

Brain Teaser #32

Answer: Neither. There are no outstanding debts between you and the bank.

There is no reason that your sum of withdrawals (which is $100) should be the same as the sum of the balances. It is purely coincidental that the right-hand balance sum is approximately $100.

For example: Suppose you withdrew $1 on 100 separate occasions; then the sum of the balances would be very large since the first few terms would be $99, $98, and $97. The sum would in fact be $5050, which is nowhere near $100. Hence, it is purely coincidental that the balance sum is near $100. It should be obvious that if your account has $100 and you withdraw it all, then there are no outstanding debts between you and the bank.

Brain Teaser #33

Answer: Yes, it is possible.

Remember history class? Paul lives in the BC era. In the BC era, successive years run from higher values to lower values until they reach 0—unlike the AD era, in which successive years run from lower values to higher values.

Most people see this riddle, think it looks backwards, and get stuck because they are naturally conditioned to think in the AD era. However, this backwardness should lead one to the right answer, since the BC era moves in the exact opposite manner to the AD era. So, Paul is born in 2000 BC, turns 15 in 1985 BC, and then five years later turns 20 in 1980 BC.

Brain Teaser #34

Answer: The more the merrier. $5.50.

People (wrongly) assume that 1998 and 1976 represent the years the coins were minted, but they are just integers. So 1998 quarters are worth $499.50 and 1976 quarters are worth $494.00, which means 1998 quarters are $5.50 more valuable than 1976 quarters.

This is the perfect puzzle to ask immediately after Brain Teaser #33 because Brain Teaser #33 conditions one to think of integers as representing years. So this puzzle tests mental flexibility, because immediately after seeing integers representing years, you must have the ability to see integers as just integers.

Brain Teaser #35

Answer: Yes. It is possible to place eight queens on a chessboard such that none of them can capture another queen.

There are twelve unique solutions. Here is one such solution:

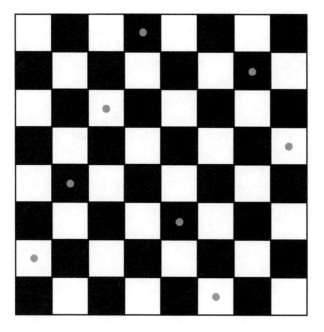

The major insight is to realize that there can only be one queen on each row and one queen on each column. Once this is realized, it becomes a matter of educated trial-and-error to find an appropriate solution.

My friend Kunal Shroff, who is at Chrysalis in Mumbai, India, asked me this puzzle. He is a great chess player, but even he took a lot of time to solve this puzzle when it was asked to him.

Brain Teaser #36

Answer: Dave should pay Barry $3 (or equivalently give him a loaf of bread).

Each loaf costs $3, so each slice is worth $1. Each soldier consumes three slices, so they all should contribute $3 in value (either with bread or cash). During the walk, Barry contributed $6 in bread, Craig contributed $3 in bread, and Dave contributed nothing. So, if Dave pays Barry $3, each in the end would have consumed three slices and paid $3 for their food. (Barry initially paid $6 to buy his two loaves of bread, but he gets a $3 payment from Dave.)

There are thousands of ways for the three soldiers to repay the debts, but the above solution is the simplest way. For example, another solution is: Barry pays Craig $1, Craig pays Barry $2, Dave pays Craig $1, and Dave pays Barry $2. Another solution is: Barry pays Craig $100, Craig pays Dave $100, and Dave pays Barry $103. In fact, there are an infinite number of possibilities because of circular payments. These circular payments occur when A pays B, B pays C, and C pays A. However, to simplify the settlements of debts, one should eliminate all circular payments.

Because the riddle asks for the simplest way to settle the debts, you must eliminate all of the circular payments, and by doing so you arrive at the answer that Dave pays Barry $3. Even though Dave takes food from Craig, he does not pay him anything at the end because of circular payments. Since Dave owes Craig money and Craig owes Barry money, you can eliminate the duplicate payments and just have Dave pay Barry (instead of having Dave pay Craig and then instantly having Craig take that money and pay Barry).

Tamara Totah, a corporate recruiter at the Oxbridge Group in New York, NY, asked me this puzzle. The concept of circular payments is used in daily activities, such as settling dinner debts, hotel bills, taxi rides, and so forth.

Brain Teaser #37

Answer: The dollar is missing because Tim and Al misallocate their strawberry sales.

In the joint venture, Tim and Al contribute strawberries at a rate of 2 for $1 and at 3 for $1, respectively. This is at first okay because this is the exact same situation as when they were selling strawberries separately. For example, in the first combined sale, Tim collects $2 for 5 strawberries. This is identical to a customer buying 2 for $1 from Tim and buying 3 for $1 from Al when they had separate shops (both situations lead to $2 for 5 strawberries). In fact, there is no problem through the tenth combined sale. But after the tenth combined sale, Al has run out of strawberries. He provides three strawberries for each sale, so he exhausts his thirty strawberries in the first ten sales. But Tim still has ten strawberries after ten combined sales, since he only uses two strawberries for each of the first ten sales.

Now, in the eleventh and twelfth sales, the ten strawberries that are sold all come from Tim's initial batch of thirty. In those two sales, $4 are collected. However, if Tim had sold these ten strawberries at his personal rate (which he should since he collected the strawberries), he would have made five sales at $1, for a total of $5. Hence, Tim is subsidizing Al in the last two sales since Al has no strawberries left, and this subsidy creates a missing dollar.

Brain Teaser #38

Answer: 11/21 (which is approximately 52.4%).

This puzzle is solved with simple algebra. Most people think you have to win 60% of the time to break even since the casino effectively has a 10% commission. But you only really need to win 52.4% of the time to break even financially.

Assume that y is the percent that you win. Then, $1-y$ is the percent you lose. So to break even, your total winnings should equal your total losses.

$$10y = 11(1-y)$$
$$10y = 11-11y$$
$$21y = 11$$
$$y = 11/21$$
$$y \cong 52.4\%$$

In the above calculations, the left-hand side of the first line represents the amount of winnings (amount won × percent of wins) and the right-hand side represents the amount of losses (amount lost × percent of losses).

So, a winning percentage of 52.4% is the break-even percentage in sports gambling. This sounds easy, but is very difficult. I don't want to waste much space here off-topic, but realize that casinos want the same amount of money bet on both the favorite and the underdog. With this situation, they don't care who wins the game and they are assured a profit. Otherwise, the casino may have an incentive for a certain team to win and this is not a situation they want to be in. For example, suppose $2.2 million is bet on Detroit and $2.2 million is bet on San Diego. The casino will then be assured of making $200,000, since it will take $2.2 million from the losers and pay the winners a total of $2.0 million. However, if there are different amounts on each team, the casino may have a chance of actually losing money. Casinos prefer as little risk as possible, so they want to equalize the amount of money bet on each team.

Sports gambling is in fact remarkably similar to money making in stocks, bonds, and commodities. Many investment and brokerage firms make money in a similar method to the manner in which sports-gambling operators make money. I have had multiple trading interviews where I impressed people with my intuitive understanding of how their firm makes money, and this intuition came from my sports-gambling interest.

Brain Teaser #39

Answer: When the rope is around either the earth or the basketball, both a mouse and a hydrogen atom could fit in the created space.

This is a highly mathematical puzzle. I only included it because the solution highlights a very interesting observation. From geometry, we remember that:

$$C = 2\pi r$$
$$r = C/2\pi$$

At first, the rope fits snugly around the equator, so the rope's length effectively represents the circumference of the earth. Also, the radius of the earth is effectively the distance from the earth's center to the rope's surface. When we add 12 inches to the rope, we effectively add 12 inches to the circumference of the earth. We now want to see the impact on the radius of the earth. Hence, we are looking for r^*, where r^* represents the new radius of the earth after the 12-inch expansion to the earth's circumference. Let C^* represent the new circumference of the earth. So:

$$r^* = C^*/2\pi$$
$$r^* = (C + 1)/2\pi \text{ (since } C^* = C + 1)$$
$$r^* = (C/2\pi) + (1/2\pi)$$
$$r^* = r + (1/2\pi)$$
$$r^* = r + 0.16$$

So we see clearly that for every foot change in the circumference of the earth, there is approximately a 0.16 feet (~2 inches) change in the radius of the earth. So when we extend our initial rope by 12 inches, there will be a 2-inch gap between the earth's surface and the rope. This is enough space for both a mouse and hydrogen atom, but not enough for a car.

Surprisingly, in the case of the basketball, the analysis is identical. The same formulas apply, and there will again be a 2-inch gap between the basketball and the rope. Again, this is enough space for both a mouse and a hydrogen atom, but not enough for a car.

The amazing takeaway from this puzzle is that regardless of the initial circular object (it could have been the sun, an apple, the moon, or even a small dot), there will always be a 2-inch gap between the object's surface and the new, extended rope.

Dorin Parasca asked this question to a group of us at the Blyth Fund (an investment club at Stanford). He was first asked this question in a trading interview at Salomon Brothers in New York, NY. Dorin is now an independent trader in Chicago, Illinois. He solved the puzzle when it was asked to him, but he used calculus to answer it. In essence, the question asks for the partial derivative of the radius with respect to change in the circumference (dr/dC). Dorin's calculus-driven solution arrives at the same answer as the geometrical solution explained above.

Brain Teaser #40

Answer: (i) 10 moves. (ii) 20 liters.

The first part's solution is:

Contents of 5-liter jug	Contents of 7-liter jug	Action
0	7	fill 7-liter jug
5	2	pour water into 5-liter jug from 7-liter jug
0	2	dump the water out of 5-liter jug
2	0	pour water from 7-liter jug into 5-liter jug
2	7	fill 7-liter jug
5	4	pour water from 7-liter jug into 5-liter jug
0	4	dump the water out of 5-liter jug
4	0	pour water from 7-liter jug into 5-liter jug
4	7	fill 7-liter jug
5	6	pour water from 7-liter jug into 5-liter jug

This solution is ten steps long. As a side note, this solution uses 21 liters of water, since the 7-liter jug is filled up three separate times.

The second part's solution is:

Contents of 5-liter jug	Contents of 7-liter jug	Action
5	0	fill 5-liter jug
0	5	pour water from 5-liter jug into 7-liter jug
5	5	fill 5-liter jug
3	7	pour water from 5-liter jug into 7-liter jug
3	0	dump the water out of 7-liter jug
0	3	pour water from 5-liter jug into 7-liter jug
5	3	fill 5-liter jug
1	7	pour water from 5-liter jug into 7-liter jug
1	0	dump the water out of 7-liter jug
0	1	pour water from 5-liter jug into 7-liter jug
5	1	fill 5-liter jug
0	6	pour water from 5-liter jug into 7-liter jug

This solution uses 20 liters of water since the 5-liter jug is filled up four times. However, this solution is two steps longer than the first solution.

I (somewhat) made up this riddle. In the movie Lethal Weapon 3, *Mel Gibson is asked this question but without consideration of the number of moves required or the amount of water used. After seeing the movie, I decided to solve the question while also minimizing the number of moves and the amount of water used.*

Brain Teaser #41

Answer: So the manhole covers won't fall through the hole.

Every other shape (including a square and an equilateral triangle) can be twisted or flipped in such a way that the heavy manhole cover could fall through the hole and into the ground. Hence, manholes are circular because this protects workers who are underneath the ground from the risk of a falling manhole cover. A secondary benefit of circular manhole covers is that they can be rolled, which makes them easy to transport.

This is an ultra-popular consulting-firm interview question. These firms like to test people's creative thinking ability. A similar question that is asked is: How can you check to see if the light in a refrigerator actually turns off when the refrigerator door is closed? This question doesn't have one right answer, but the firms are looking for creative solutions such as: (1) build a life-size refrigerator model and sit inside of it while the door is closed; (2) place light-sensitive items in the refrigerator and measure their characteristics immediately after opening the door; (3) calculate the average life-span of a light bulb, then close the door for at least that amount of time, and then open the door and see if the light bulb still works; or (4) drill a peephole on the side of the refrigerator.

Brain Teaser #42

Answer: $2/3$ (approximately 67%).

I will present two solutions. The first is straightforward and uses a lot of math. The second is more elegant.

One way to solve this is to analyze every scenario in which Tom wins. There are multiple such scenarios. If he initially flips a head, the sequence is H, and he wins. His next possible winning sequence is TTH. After that, it is TTTTH. This continues forever. So mathematically, the probability that Tom wins is:

$$P \text{ (Tom wins)} = 1/2 + 1/8 + 1/32 + 1/128 + \ldots$$
$$= \text{Sigma } (1/2)^n, \text{ where } n \text{ is all odd integers.}$$
$$= \text{first term } / (1 - \text{term factor})$$
$$= (1/2)/[1 - (1/4)]$$
$$= (1/2)/(3/4)$$
$$= 2/3$$

The first line is the sum of each of Tom's chances to win. On every flip, there is a 50% chance of a head and a 50% chance of a tail. So, for example, for TTH to occur, the probability sequence is $1/2 \times 1/2 \times 1/2 = 1/8$. To go from the second line to the third line, we realize that the second line is an infinite geometric sequence with a term factor of $1/4$ (the term factor is the ratio of successive terms). From algebra, we remember that a sum of an infinite geometric sequence $= \text{(first term)}/(1 - \text{term factor})$. Simple arithmetic then leads to an answer of $2/3$.

The more elegant solution uses little math. Assume Tom's probability of initially winning is x. Now, suppose Tom's first flip is a tail. Now, at this point, we know that Jill's chance of winning is also x (since she is now in the same situation that Tom was in prior to his first flip). However, the situation in which Jill gets to flip occurs only 50% of the time since there is a 50% chance that Tom initially flips a head and ends the game. So, Jill's initial chance of winning is $1/2x$, since there is a 50% chance that she gets to the situation in which her probability of winning is x and there is a 50% chance she will lose on Tom's first flip. Either Tom or Jill must win. We know Tom's initial chance of winning is x and Jill's is $1/2x$, so that means $x + 1/2x = 1$ (someone must win). Simple algebra leads to $x = 2/3$. Since x is defined as Tom's chance of winning, he has a $2/3$ probability of winning.

This is a popular puzzle, often asked by venture capital firms, high tech firms, and investment banks. In my opinion, interviewers are satisfied with the right answer, since it is a tough puzzle. So when someone uses brute mathematical force to solve it, he or she has done well. But there are thousands of students who graduate with math and engineering degrees each year. The interviewer is much more impressed when someone uses a creative solution (such as the second solution) because it demonstrates the ability to "think outside the box."

Brain Teaser #43

Answer: This is possible, so Larry is telling the truth.

There are two critical elements in this puzzle: leap year and the International Date Line. Jim was born on March 1, just west of the International Date Line. His mother then crossed the International Date Line and gave birth to Larry. This happened in a non-leap year, so as the mother crossed the Date Line, the day falls back from March 1 to February 28. So, Jim is born on March 1 and Larry on February 28.

Today it is February 28 in a leap year. So, Larry's birthday is today. Jim's birthday is in two days (since tomorrow is February 29). Also, Larry is younger than Jim even though Jim's birthday is first, since we defined younger to mean born after and Larry was born after Jim.

I overheard this riddle in a shopping center in Providence, Rhode Island.

Brain Teaser #44

Answer: 450 miles.

The straightforward, but practically impossible, method of solving this question is to calculate each segment the bee travels and then add up all of the segments to arrive at a total distance traveled. However, this is very tedious and requires a lot of algebra.

There is a more elegant solution. The bee is always traveling at 75 mph (regardless of whether it is going toward San Francisco or toward Los Angeles). So by definition, in every hour of time, the bee travels 75 miles. The trains are initially 600 miles apart and they get 100 miles closer to each other every hour, because Train ABC moves 40 miles north every hour and Train XYZ moves 60 miles south every hour. Hence, it will take exactly six hours for the trains to collide. If the bee is traveling for 6 hours at its rate of 75 mph, then the bee must travel a total distance of 450 miles.

My friend Annu Jindal asked me this riddle between pickup basketball games many years ago. Annu is currently at Michigan Law School.

Brain Teaser #45

Part 1 answer:
Chicago White Sox (MLB)
Boston Red Sox (MLB)
Orlando Magic (NBA)
Miami Heat (NBA)
Utah Jazz (NBA)

Most people quickly answer White Sox and Red Sox. The others are more difficult, though Magic and Heat are often answered together since both are expansion basketball teams from Florida. One decoy is that there are no football teams in the list. This is my all-time favorite sports trivia puzzle because it seems very easy to answer, but often takes a very long time.

Part 2 answer:
Cardinals (Arizona and St. Louis)
Giants (New York and San Francisco)
Kings (Sacramento and Los Angeles)
Rangers (Texas and New York)
Panthers (Carolina and Florida)

This is another favorite sports riddle because it also seems easy, but is deceivingly difficult.

Brain Teaser #46

Answer: Yes.

The question can be reduced to its fundamentals with a few simple steps. The first phrase ("If the puzzle you solved before you solved the puzzle you solved after you solved the puzzle you solved before you solved this one") can be rephrased as, "If the puzzle you solved before you solved this one." The second phrase ("was harder than the puzzle you solved after you solved the puzzle you solved before you solve this one") can be rephrased as, "was harder than this one." So, we can rephrase the whole questions as: "If the puzzle you solved before you solved this one was harder than this one, was the puzzle you solved before this one harder than this one?" This is a rhetorical question—the answer is yes.

Brain Teaser #47

Answer: 21/32 (approximately 66%).

This puzzle can be solved by several methods, the easiest of which is brute force. I generally try to present the most elegant solutions to the puzzles in this book, but in certain situations, I believe that brute force is the best solution (when an elegant solution risks conceptual error).

After six pitches have been tossed, it is possible to determine whether there is a strikeout or a walk. If there are already three strikes, it is a strikeout; otherwise it is a walk.

There are two equally likely choices for each of the six pitches (S or B), so there is a total of 64 equally likely possibilities. In shorthand notation, I list below every strikeout scenario. I say shorthand because in some cases a strikeout is determined before the sixth pitch, and in those cases I simply list the number of times such a case occurs in the first column. However, it is critical to understand that these situations should be counted multiple times since they occur more often than other scenarios.

	Pitch #					
Occurrences	1	2	3	4	5	6
8	S	S	S			
4	S	S	B	S		
4	S	B	S	S		
4	B	S	S	S		
2	S	S	B	B	S	
2	S	B	S	B	S	
2	S	B	B	S	S	
2	B	S	S	B	S	
2	B	S	B	S	S	
2	B	B	S	S	S	
1	S	S	B	B	B	S
1	S	B	S	B	B	S
1	S	B	B	S	B	S
1	S	B	B	B	S	S
1	B	S	S	B	B	S
1	B	S	B	S	B	S
1	B	S	B	B	S	S
1	B	B	S	S	B	S
1	B	B	S	B	S	S
1	B	B	B	S	S	S

A count shows there are 42 strikeout possibilities. Since there are a total of 64 outcomes, the probability of a strikeout is 42/64, which reduces to 21/32 (approximately 66%).

The common pitfall in this puzzle is to count each of the above situations only once. However, they should be weighted differently. For example, the SSS case should be counted 8 times. This is because the SSS case occurs 8 times as much as other unique cases (such as BBBSSS). In reality, the SSS is shorthand for the following 8 separate cases: SSSSSS, SSSSSB, SSSSBS, SSSBSS, SSSSBB, SSSBSB, SSSBBS, and SSSBBB. Each of these 8 cases occurs as frequently as BBBSSS, so the shorthand SSS case should be counted 8 times. This logic applies to the 4× and 2× shorthand cases as well.

This question was on the second round of the Michigan Math Prize Competition in my junior year of high school. The test consisted of five questions with an allotted 3 hours (so each question should take about 36 minutes). I luckily got this question with brute force, but did much more poorly on the other questions.

Brain Teaser #48

Answer: The letter *e*.

This is a great puzzle to ask after bombarding someone with several mathematical puzzles. Once people focus on math and analytical concepts, it is difficult to utilize verbal logic skills.

Brain Teaser #49

Answer:

Oliver—sailor and scuba diver.
Olga—biker and swimmer.
Oscar—golfer and skateboarder.

A systematic and educated trial-and-error method is the most efficient process to solve this puzzle.

From the sixth clue, it is evident that Oliver is the sailor. Now, from the first, second, and fourth clues, we see that Oliver is not the golfer, biker, skateboarder, or swimmer. So, he must also be the scuba diver. The fifth clue tells us that Olga is not the golfer, so that means Oscar is the golfer. Now, from the first clue, we see that Olga is the biker. Now, from the third clue, we see that Oscar is also the skateboarder. By default, that means Olga is also the swimmer.

Mark Blumling presented me with a similar version of this puzzle a few years ago. Mark is currently at Stanford Law School.

Brain Teaser #50

Answer: Gary wins again.

From the first race it is evident that Gary runs 50 yards in the same time that Barry runs 45 yards. Since they maintain the same speeds in the second race, Gary and Barry will be side-to-side with 5 yards to go since Gary would have run 50 yards and Barry 45 yards. Since we know that Gary is a faster runner, he will finish ahead of Barry in the remaining 5 yards.

Tricky Twenty #1

Answer: Pirate A suggests 98-0-1-0-1. His suggestion passes with Pirates A, C, and E voting yes and Pirates B and D voting no.

This is a classic puzzle. Most people initially attack it by seeing how each pirate would react on a random suggestion given by A. For example, people try to figure out what happens if A suggests 40-25-25-0-10. Who would vote for this? Assume that A and E vote for it. A votes for it because he wants to stay alive and E is happy to get 10 coins since he is the most junior pirate. Would B and C vote for this? You could argue no, since B could easily scheme with C and tell him that they should both vote no and after A is thrown to death, B would suggest 50-50-0-0. This suggestion of 50-50-0-0 would pass if both B and C voted yes and this would yield more coins to both B and C than the original proposal. However, one could counter-argue that C might not believe in B's scheme, since if C does vote against A's initial proposal of 40-25-25-0-10, B could break his promise and suggest 80-0-5-15 (and not give C his promised 50 coins). Since B is greedy, he would be willing to break his promise to C because he wants as many coins as possible. But since B is also intelligent, he would only do this if he knew he would stay alive (i.e., he knows D and/or E would vote yes to his new proposal). So maybe C would vote yes for A's initial suggestion because he doesn't trust B. But wait a minute. Maybe C should scheme with D and/or E. If he gets those two on his side, they could all vote against both A's and B's suggestion and then split the coins just among the three of them. So does that mean B does not take any risk and vote yes for A's initial suggestion? How about E—does he now vote no for the original suggestion? As you can see, it is easy to get trapped into circular logic streams when trying to solve this puzzle from the front end.

The insight is to use backward induction (i.e., solving the puzzle by starting at the end). Suppose that A, B, and C have already been thrown overboard to death. Now D is about to make a suggestion. He is intelligent and greedy. Hence, he will for sure suggest 100-0. He will vote yes and E will vote no. Since it is a tie, it will pass. So we know for sure that if there are two pirates remaining, the game ends with D getting 100 coins and E getting 0 coins.

Now suppose that only A and B have been thrown overboard. So now C is about to make a suggestion. He will for sure suggest 99-0-1. C and E will vote yes and D will vote no. E will vote yes because if he doesn't, he knows that he will for sure get 0 coins in the next round (100-0). D can't make any promises to E to persuade him to vote no, since any such promise is not credible. Thus, C only needs to offer one coin to ensure that E votes yes.

(C can't suggest 100-0-0 because that does not give E a compelling reason to vote yes). Since C is intelligent and greedy, he will give just one coin to E. So we know for sure that if there are three pirates remaining, the game ends with C getting 99, D getting 0, and E getting 1.

Now suppose that only A has been thrown overboard. So now B is about to make a suggestion. He will for sure suggest 99-0-1-0. B and D will vote yes and C and E will vote no. It is a tie, so it passes. D will vote yes because if he doesn't, he knows that he will for sure get 0 coins in the next round (99-0-1). C can't make any credible promises to D to convince him otherwise. Again, B only needs to offer 1 coin to D to ensure he votes yes. So we know for sure that if there are four pirates remaining, the game ends with B getting 99, C getting 0, D getting 1, and E getting 0.

Since all of the pirates are intelligent, all of them, including A, easily solve for the above logic. So, at the beginning, A will for sure suggest 98-0-1-0-1. A, C, and E will vote yes and B and D will vote no. C and E will vote yes because if they don't, they know for sure they will get 0 coins in the next round (99-0-1-0). As before, B can't make any credible promises to convince them otherwise. Again, A has to give C and E just 1 coin each to ensure a yes vote from each of them.

Hence the only equilibrium solution is A's suggestion of 98-0-1-0-1, which passes with a 3-2 vote.

Some critics argue that C and/or E would vote no in order to spite A. They argue that the difference between 0 and 1 coin is small and thus C and/or E would vote no just so A is thrown to death. However, this is flawed logic. C and E are greedy, which means they will try to maximize their personal wealth. Hence, they will accept one coin. They may not be happy with this outcome, but they are intelligent and greedy so they will vote yes.

Likewise, A can't offer 100-0-0-0-0. This is because C and E don't have a compelling reason to vote yes. A is intelligent, so he won't risk a situation which may very likely lead to his death. He would like to get all 100 coins, but he needs to entice C and E with 1 coin each to ensure a yes vote.

This puzzle was asked to me in a trading interview at Goldman Sachs. It was a popular riddle among firms during the 1996 recruiting season. It is popular among traders especially because it involves both corner situation thinking and backward induction.

Tricky Twenty #2

Answer: 17 minutes.

There are two possible solutions. Here is the first such solution:

Action	Time
A and B cross over	2 min
A comes back	1 min
C and D cross over	10 min
B comes back	2 min
A and B cross over	2 min
Total:	17 min

The second solution is the same as the first solution, except that Person B comes back in the second step and Person A comes back in the fourth step.

Most people quickly arrive at an answer of 19 minutes. This is because they (wrongly) assume that the correct answer involves Person A escorting the other three people across the bridge by shuffling back and forth. The logic insight is to realize that it is possible to get both Person C and Person D across the bridge on a single trip without having one of them to return the flashlight.

This puzzle was supposedly asked to all candidates at Microsoft in the 1998 recruiting season. Today, this puzzle is still used by several technology firms and venture capital firms. (A group of twelve software engineers at a Fortune 500 firm supposedly took three days to solve this puzzle.)

Tricky Twenty #3

Answer: 21.

This is a difficult puzzle. You should first realize that there are only 43 different answers my dad could have possibly heard, namely the numbers 0–42 inclusive. This is because the fewest number of hands anyone could have shaken is 0 and the most is 42 (since there are 44 people and no one shakes their own hand or their spouse's hand). My dad asked 43 people the question, so each of the 43 must have given him a different answer from 0 to 42.

For the sake of explanation, assume that the 21 couples besides my parents are: (1) Woman A, Man A, (2) Woman B, Man B, (3) Woman C, Man C, . . . , (20) Woman T, Man T, and (21) Woman U, Man U.

I will show that my mom could not have said either 0 or 42. If she had said 0, then it would have been impossible for anyone to give an answer of 42. This is because nobody would have shaken his or her own hand, their spouse's hand, or my mom's hand (since my mom said 0), which leaves only 41 hands remaining. So, my mom could not have said 0. Similarly, she could not have said 42. If she had said 42, nobody could have given an answer of 0 (since my mom would have shaken everyone's hand besides her own and my dad's). So, my mom could not have said 42 either.

So someone besides my mom must have said 42. Let's assume this is Woman A (it will become evident it doesn't matter if I choose Woman A or Man A). So, if Woman A gives an answer of 42, she must have shaken the hands of everyone in the other 21 couples (including my parents), which means no one within those 21 couples could have answered 0 (since they all shake Woman A's hand). So, Man A must have answered 0. Please observe that the person who answered 42 (Woman A) is married to the person who answered 0 (Man A).

I will now show that my mom could not have said either 1 or 41. If she had said one, she must have shaken hands with Woman A. But that would imply no one else could have said 41. This is because without one's own hand, their spouse's hand, Man A's hand, and my mom's hand, there are only 40 hands remaining. So my mom could not have answered one. Similarly, if she had said 41, she would have shaken hands with everyone except herself, my dad, and Man A. But that means that nobody else could have said one (since everyone else would have shaken hands with my mom and Woman A). So, my mom could not have said 41 either.

So someone besides my mom must have said 41. Let's assume this is Woman B (again it is irrelevant if I choose Woman B or Man B). So, if Woman B gives an answer of 41, she must have shaken hands with everyone except herself, her spouse, and Man A. This means that Man B must have said one (since everyone else shakes hands with at least Woman A and Woman B). Man B must have only shaken hands with Woman A and nobody else. Please observe that the person who answered 41 (Woman B) is married to the person who answered 1 (Man B).

We now know the following: (1) Woman A said 42, (2) Man A said 0, (3) Woman B said 41, and (4) Man B said 1. Now we can easily show that my mom did not say either 40 or 2, by using the same logic from above. Then, if we assume that Woman C said 40, we can show that Man C must have said 2, by again using the logic from above.

By furthering the logic from above, it becomes crystal clear that every couple's handshakes must add up to 42 for the situation described in the puzzle to exist (i.e., the situation in which my dad hears each number between 0 and 42 once). This means that my mom (and dad) shake 21 hands. Intuitively, you can keep matching couples (42-0, 41-1, 40-2, 39-3, 38-4, . . . , 23-19, 22-20) until the only available number for my mom to answer is 21. On a side note, it is easy to prove that the 21 hands my mom shakes are the same 21 hands that my dad shakes.

The easiest method of attacking this puzzle is to start with a smaller number of couples. For example, suppose only four couples were at the party (with the exact same conditions), it is easy to show with pencil and paper that my mom must have shaken three hands and the other three couples have handshakes that all total to six (6-0, 5-1, and 4-2). This minipuzzle can be solved with trial and error, since so few combinations exist. After solving this minipuzzle, the logic should become apparent, and then the solution to the actual puzzle should come naturally.

Nick Burgin, a Princeton graduate, asked me this puzzle. He was a colleague of mine at Goldman Sachs, but he now trades at a small, proprietary operation in Tokyo, Japan. He sent the puzzle to me on e-mail one night. I tried using Excel to solve it, but quickly got frustrated. The next morning in the shower, I came up with the insight needed to solve the puzzle.

Tricky Twenty #4

Answer: The ages are: 2, 2, and 9.

After Kramer provides the first clue, Jose calculates that there are only eight possible combinations, namely:

1, 1, and 36
1, 2, and 18
1, 3, and 12
1, 4, and 9
1, 6, and 6
2, 2, and 9
2, 3, and 6
3, 3, and 4

So after the first clue Jose has narrowed the answer to one of the above possibilities. But he doesn't know which is the right answer, so he asks for another clue.

Kramer gives him the second clue (sum of ages). After looking at the address, Jose still doesn't know the answer, thus he asks for yet another clue. Suppose the address was 38. Jose wouldn't need another clue, since he would know the solution is 1, 1, and 36. Suppose the address was 21. Again, Jose wouldn't need another clue, since he would know the solution is 1, 2, and 18. However, the address is 13. This is the only number that requires Jose to ask for another clue, since two different combinations (1, 6 and 6 and 2, 2, and 9) both add up to 13. If the address were any number besides 13, Jose would have right away figured out the three ages and would not have asked for a third clue. However, since he does ask for a third clue, we know the address is 13, thereby leaving two potential solutions.

Kramer gives the third clue, which indicates that there are two children who are both younger than the older child (since they both wear the old clothes of the eldest child). This means that the two older children are not twins. This eliminates the 1, 6, and 6 combination. By default, Jose realizes that the ages must be 2, 2, and 9.

I was asked this riddle at a summer camp when I was in high school.

Tricky Twenty #5

Answer: One time.

Most people assume that you should stack five files on the scale on the first weigh. This narrows the cheater to a stack of five. Then, they argue that you put either two or three on the scale (which narrows the cheater to a stack of three). This line of logic requires four uses of the balance scale.

There is a much faster way to catch the cheating supplier. Take one coin from the first supplier, two coins from the second supplier, three coins from the third supplier, . . . , nine coins from the ninth supplier, and ten coins from the tenth supplier. So you have a total of 55 coins. Without any cheaters, the balance should read 550 ounces with these coins.

However, the balance reading will be lower since there is a cheater. The actual reading will determine which of the suppliers is the cheater. For example, suppose the balance reads 548 ounces. This means that of the 55 coins, two are light 9-ounce coins, which means the second supplier is the cheater. Instead, suppose the balance reads 543 ounces. This means there are seven light 9-ounce coins, which means the seventh supplier is the cheater. You will for sure receive a reading between 540 and 549. The value of the scale will indicate who is the cheating supplier.

Savan Patel, who runs Excell Electronics in Chicago, Illinois, asked me this question. This is tricky, especially since most other scale riddles use balance scales, not bathroom-style pointer scales. During one interview, I answered an easy balance scale riddle from a very rude interviewer. He then challenged me to stump him. I asked him this riddle, and he failed miserably (he thought the answer was four). He now supposedly uses this riddle in all of his interviews.

Tricky Twenty #6

Answer: 8/26 (which is approximately 30.8%).

The easiest method of solving this puzzle is to assume the firm interviews 100 people. Any number will arrive at a solution of 8/26, but 100 is chosen for ease of calculation. Of the 100 people, 10 candidates are good, and since the firm is 80% accurate, it will rightly deem 8 of the 10 to be good (and hire these 8) and wrongly deem 2 to be bad (and not hire these 2). The other 90 candidates are bad, and since the firm is 80% accurate, it will rightly deem 72 to be bad (and not hire these 72) and wrongly deem 18 to be good (and hire these 18). So, in total the firm will hire 26 people, 8 of whom are qualified and 18 of whom are not. Thus, 8/26 is the percentage of hired employees that are truly qualified candidates.

Leveraged buyouts (LBOs) often ask this puzzle to potential hires. I too was asked this question (but not for an LBO position), and I failed miserably on the question. I kept thinking the answer was 80%—which is what most people answer. However, an 80% answer would imply that the 10% statistic is an irrelevant figure. This can't be the case. Intuitively, if the 10% figure were 0% or 100%, it would then be obvious that either none or all of the hired employees would be good (which proves that the 10% figure does play a part in the calculation). I was unable even to solve for this logical step in the solution and adamantly believed the solution was 80%. No wonder I didn't get a second-round interview.

In fact, the 10% statistic is the reason that even though the firm is pretty good at assessing candidates, the percentage of good hired people is so low. Since so little of the population is qualified (10%), there are lots of candidates (90%) on which the firm can make a mistake and wrongly hire.

Tricky Twenty #7

Answer: You should definitely switch doors. This will increase your probability of winning the car from 1/3 to 2/3.

At first glance, it seems that it does not matter whether you stay or switch because both remaining doors have an equal probability of having the car and the goat. This logic is, however, flawed.

If you stay with the original door, you will win whenever you initially selected a car (1/3 of the time) and you will lose when you initially selected a goat (2/3 of the time). However, if you switch doors, you will win whenever you initially selected a goat (2/3 of the time) and you will lose when you initially selected a car (1/3 of the time). So, this shows that you will increase your chances of winning from 1/3 to 2/3 by switching doors since staying has a 1/3 chance of winning and switching has a 2/3 chance of winning.

This solution is confusing and unsettling. It naturally seems that there is a 50-50 chance of either the car or the goat since there are two unopened doors and two unknown items. An important idea that helps explain this solution is that sometimes your uncle has a choice in which door to show and sometimes he is forced to show a particular door. More specifically, when you initially select the car, your uncle can show either door (since both have goats). But, when you initially select a goat, he has to show you a particular door (the one with the other goat). This asymmetry helps explain the asymmetrical answer. Most people think there is perfect symmetry in the puzzle, and therefore wrongly believe the solution is also symmetrical.

There are numerous stories in which college professors have argued about the solution to this riddle, arguing (wrongly) that once you see the goat, it becomes a 50-50 proposition. If you still don't believe the answer, simply play the game by having someone else act as your uncle and have him or her select the original locations of the car and goats. If you play enough times, you will empirically see that switching leads to a 2/3 success rate while staying is only successful 1/3 of the time.

This is an old-time favorite brain teaser that has circulated for many years. In college, my economics professor brought in three boxes; two were empty and the other had 10 points of free extra credit in it. The student who won our class investing competition was allowed to select a box. After he picked a box, the professor showed him an empty box and offered him the option to stay with his original box or to switch to the other unknown box. Our whole class yelled at him to switch, since many of us had seen this puzzle before, but he decided to stay with his original selection. He ended up winning the extra credit—I guess it is better to be lucky than smart.

Tricky Twenty #8

Answer: Yes, you can escape to freedom.

Suppose the radius of the lake is r. Understand that a straight path will fail, because you have r to travel and the robber has at most πr to travel. Since he is four times faster, he will be able to travel πr faster than you travel r (since π is approximately 3.14).

You need to move $r/4$ away from the center in any direction. For simplicity, assume you move toward the robber (so he does not move). You then start rowing clockwise in a circle. The robber will be able to move at exactly the same angular speed as you—since he is traveling four times the distance at four times the speed. Hence, he will maintain his strategic position on shore (i.e., he will continue to always be at the point on shore that is closest to you). Now, you drop down to a slightly smaller radius, say $r/4.01$. You will now be going faster than the robber, and the angle lead that you have on him will gradually grow as you row in a circle. Since, the robber always moves in the optimal direction, he will try to stay at the closest point on shore from you, but he will continue to get further and further from that point since your angular speed is greater than his. Wait until you have a 180° lead (or just slightly before that point). Then, change your direction and head straight for the shore. You have a distance of $3r/4$ to cover and he has a distance of πr to cover. He has more than four times the distance that you have, so you will get to shore without him being there, thereby ensuring your escape. (On a side note, the robber will switch directions when your angular lead becomes greater than 180°.)

I was given this riddle at a fixed-income trading interview at Goldman Sachs. I was not able to solve it on the spot, but luckily got the job anyway.

Tricky Twenty #9

Answer: Yes.

Label the balls 1 through 12. On the first try, weigh 1-2-3-4 versus 5-6-7-8.

If they balance, then the odd ball is among 9-10-11-12. On the second try, weigh 9-10-11 versus 1-2-3. If they balance, the odd ball is 12. Then, on the third try, place any of the good balls (1-11) versus 12 to determine whether 12 is heavier or lighter. If on the second try there is an imbalance, then the odd ball is among 9-10-11. The direction of the scale will indicate if the odd ball is heavier or lighter. Then, on the third try, weigh 9 versus 10. If they balance, 11 is the odd ball (and you already know whether it is heavier or lighter). Otherwise, if they don't balance, it is obvious whether 9 or 10 is the odd ball (since you already know whether the odd ball is heavier or lighter).

If on the first try (1-2-3-4 versus 5-6-7-8), there is an imbalance, we know the odd ball is within these 8 balls. Assume 1-2-3-4 moves downward (it's irrelevant which direction it moves, but for explanation's sake assume it moves downward). This means that either 1-2-3-4 is heavy or 5-6-7-8 is light. Now, on the second try, weigh 1-2-5 versus 3-4-6. If 1-2-5 moves downward, then either 1 or 2 is heavy or 6 is light. Then, on the third try, weigh 1 versus 2 and it should be evident which of the balls (1, 2, or 6) is the odd ball and whether it is heavy or light. However, if on the second try (1-2-5 versus 3-4-6), the 3-4-6 side moves downward, then either 3 or 4 is heavy or 5 is light. Then, on the third try weigh 3 versus 4 and it should be evident which of the balls (3, 4, or 5) is the odd ball and whether it is heavy or light. If on the second try (1-2-5 versus 3-4-6), there is a balance, then either 7 or 8 is the odd ball (and we know it is light from the first weigh). Then, on the third try, weigh 7 versus 8, and it should be evident which is the odd, light ball.

The above schematic proves that you can determine which is the odd ball and whether it is heavy or light within three weighs.

The major logical insight is to realize that the balls should be split into three groups before the first weigh. If you were to weigh 1–6 versus 7–12 on the first weigh, you would not eliminate any balls (since you don't know if the odd ball is heavy or light). So you must divide the balls into 3 groups.

Nikhil Chanani, a friend of mine who is now at Harvard Medical School, asked me this puzzle during a computer science class at Stanford. He was originally asked this puzzle by his friend Peter Chen, who now works at Epiphany.

Tricky Twenty #10

Answer: Yes, you can measure 45 minutes.

At the same time, burn both ends of the first rope and burn one end of the second rope. When the flames of the first rope meet, which will happen somewhere in between the two ends (but not necessarily in the exact middle), light the unlit end of the second rope. Now, when the flames of the second rope meet, exactly 45 minutes will have elapsed from the time the ropes first started to burn.

This solution is somewhat difficult to conceptualize, because the ropes do not necessarily burn at a uniform rate—this means that one small segment of the rope may take 59 minutes to burn and the rest of it only take 1 minute. You know that a single flame takes exactly one hour to burn across each rope. So, if there are two flames burning toward each other, it must take 30 minutes for them to meet. This will always happen. It may happen near the middle or near one of the ends, depending on how the rope burns across its surface, but for sure it will be 30 minutes when the flames meet. Another way to think of this is to think of the two flames in sequential order (although in reality they are simultaneous). We know that in sequence the total time of the two flames would be one hour since the rope takes an hour to burn. We know in reality that there are simultaneous flames that start and end at the same time, so each flame must have burned for exactly 30 minutes.

So when the second rope has its second end lit as well, there are 30 total minutes of rope to be burned (since a single flame has been already been lit for the last 30 minutes). Using the same logic as above, it is easy to show that the two flames will meet in exactly 15 additional minutes (regardless of each individual flame's rate). Again, you can think of the two flames occurring in sequence—and you know that the total sequence will take exactly 30 minutes. But, in reality they occur at the same time for the same length of time, so that means 15 more minutes must have elapsed.

Thus, 45 minutes can be measured with the two ropes. Many people try to tear, slice, or rip the rope. However, this adds no value since the rope does not necessarily burn at a uniform rate (i.e., tearing it in half does not ensure that each half takes 30 minutes to burn).

Hemanth Parasuram, a business development manager at Tibco Software, asked me this puzzle. I sampled this puzzle among my friends and surprisingly almost nobody was able to solve it within 15 minutes. This was surprising to me because there are not that many different ways to burn the two ropes, so I would have expected more people to solve the riddle quickly by simple trial and error.

Tricky Twenty #11

Answer: It is impossible to draw—that is, there are zero solutions.

One simple insight makes this puzzle trivial, even though at first glance the puzzle seems extremely difficult. Each domino, regardless of its location, will always cover one white square and one black square. Initially, there are 32 white squares and 32 black squares, so the 32 dominoes easily fit onto the 64 squares.

Now, two black squares are removed (the opposite corner squares). So now there are 31 dominoes, 30 black squares, and 32 white squares. It is impossible for the 31 dominoes to cover the 32 white squares. With 30 dominoes, you can cover all the black squares and 30 of the white squares. But this leaves one unusable domino and two uncovered white squares. Hence, the puzzle is impossible to solve, since there always will be at least two uncovered white squares.

If you were trying to solve this without the black/white strategy, it would be very difficult to do. I was asked the puzzle without a chessboard in front of me. I was completely stumped. However, when I went home and pulled out a standard black-and-white chessboard, I was able to solve the puzzle immediately. This question underscores the importance of pattern recognition (colors, numbers, etc.) in problem solving.

On a side note, this puzzle is always solvable if the two removed squares consist of one white and one black square (regardless of the location of the removed white and black squares).

Tricky Twenty #12

Answer: Colin knows that he has a red hat on because neither Larry nor Gene figures out the color of his hat instantaneously.

Let us first understand the initial dilemma. As soon as the three contestants open their eyes, each sees two red hats. So they all raise their hands. Now, each contestant sees two red hats and two raised hands (and their own hands are also raised). Now, each tries to figure out if they have a red or green hat. The problem for each contestant is that regardless of whether he has a red or green hat, the situation would be identical (i.e., seeing two red hats, seeing two raised hands, and having his own hand raised).

For example, Colin initially sees two red hats and two raised hands. Suppose Colin has a red hat, the other two students would obviously have their hands raised. But even if Colin had a green hat (which he doesn't), the other two students would still be raising their hands (since they see each other's red hats). In reality everyone sees two red hats, so each contestant knows that the only possible scenarios are: (1) three red hats or (2) two red hats and one green hat (with the green hat on their own head since they personally see the other two red hats). Thus, initially all three students are in a stalemate situation unable to figure out their own hat's color (since with the information given and deduced they can't distinguish between the two possible scenarios).

The brilliant insight is to incorporate the reactions of the other two contestants. Let's take Colin's perspective. He sees two red hats and two raised hands. Suppose he had a green hat. Then, Larry would be raising his hand because of Gene's red hat and Gene would be raising his hand because of Larry's red hat. Now, if Colin did have a green hat, both Larry and Gene would instantaneously figure out the color of their own hats. Here's why. If Colin had a green hat, Larry would see Gene's raised hand and Colin's green hat, so Larry would know that Gene is raising his hand because Gene sees Larry's red hat. So if Colin had a green hat, Larry would be able to solve the puzzle within seconds and would immediately leave the room. (The same logic applies to Gene. He would immediately realize that Larry is raising his hand because Larry sees Gene's red hat. So if Colin's hat were green, Larry and Gene would be racing out the door right away.)

However, in reality, there is no initial movement by the contestants (the puzzle mentions that each sits and thinks for a minute). Colin realizes that the only reason nobody is walking out is because everyone is in the same dilemma (i.e., seeing two red rats and two raised hands). Otherwise, as the above analysis shows, Larry and/or Gene would be racing to the door. Since everyone sees two red hats, no one is able to solve the puzzle immediately. Therefore, Colin walks out and explains that he must have a red hat since his competitors did not immediately solve the puzzle. In other words, the only possible situation that can stump all three contestants for more than a few milliseconds is when everyone has a red hat.

Tricky Twenty #13

Answer: Yes, Shannon is correct. There is only one solution to the equation and it can be found without trial and error.

A few mathematical insights make the solution obvious. Whenever two digits are brought down in the division, there must be a 0 in the quotient. This occurs twice—once before and once after the 8. So, we know the quotient takes the form of x080x.

In the last step, the divisor is multiplied by some digit to arrive at a four-digit number. This digit must be 9. This is because when the divisor is multiplied by 8 (done previously since 8 appears in the quotient earlier), the product is only a three-digit number. So, the quotient's last digit is a 9 and therefore it must take the form of x0809.

The divisor can't be more than 125, because 125 multiplied by 8 yields a four-digit number (and we know that the divisor multiplied by 8 is a three-digit number). Also, the quotient's first digit must be greater than 7. This is because 7 multiplied by any number less than 125 would leave more than a two-digit remainder when subtracted by the first four digits of the dividend (the first four dividend digits can't be less than 1000 and $7 \times 124 = 868$, which would lead to a three-digit remainder of 132). We also know that the first digit in the quotient can't be 9, since 9 multiplied by the divisor gives us a four-digit number (from above analysis). So, the first digit is an 8. Therefore, the quotient must be 80809.

Now, we can easily see that the divisor must be greater than 123. This is because 123 x 80809 yields a seven-digit product and our dividend has eight digits. Since our divisor also must be less than 125 (from above analysis), we know that the divisor must be 124.

So, the quotient is 80809, the divisor is 124, and the dividend must be 10020316. This means the only possible calculation is:

```
              80809
      124 / 10020316
            992
            ‾‾‾‾
            1003
             992
            ‾‾‾‾
            1116
            1116
            ‾‾‾‾
               0
```

A form of this riddle is considered the most famous and difficult problem ever published in The American Mathematical Monthly, *a magazine known for its challenging puzzles. P. L. Chessin submitted this problem in 1954 to the magazine when he was working for Westinghouse Electric Corporation.*

I was asked a simpler version of this problem in an interview. I luckily solved it since I had earlier seen this more complicated puzzle. This puzzle tests one's ability to analyze corner situations. The trader was impressed with my solution and was even more impressed when I asked him this puzzle (which he was able to solve). Yet, unfortunately I still didn't get the job offer.

Tricky Twenty #14

Answer: 10 units.

There are two diagonals of the rectangle, namely BD and AC. AC is also equal to the radius of the circle. From the diagram, we see that AE, which is also the radius of the circle, is 10 units long. Therefore, AC is also 10 units. From elementary geometry, we remember that both diagonals of a rectangle are equal in length. Therefore, BD is equal to AC, which means BD is also 10 units.

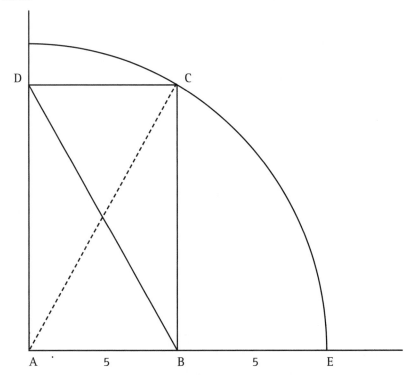

I am very fond of this puzzle because it appears to require a lot of geometry and algebra knowledge, but in reality requires common sense. I have never seen this particular question on a standardized test, but this is typical of the more difficult math questions that are found on the SAT, the GMAT, and the GRE.

My sister Sindhu asked me this puzzle after she spotted it in a magazine.

Tricky Twenty #15

Answer: The Norwegian drinks water. The Japanese owns the Zebra.

There is no simple shortcut. This puzzle requires educated trial-and-error. From clues 9, 10, and 15, we see that:

	House 1	House 2	House 3	House 4	House 5
Color				Blue	
Nationality	Norwegian				
Drink					Milk
Cigarette					
Pet					

With the use of other clues, you can eliminate certain combinations. You then need to make some assumptions (such as House 3 is ivory) and see if you reach an inconsistency. If you do, you start over. Eventually you will arrive at the correct solution.

I will not outline my complete methodology, since there are an infinite number of approaches, none necessarily being better prima facie than the others. Some assumptions do lead to the solution more quickly, but there is no way to know this before making the assumption. I tried resolving this puzzle using a grid (which contained every combination), but it was too cumbersome and my belief is it is much quicker to solve using educated trial and error.

The complete scenario is:

	House 1	House 2	House 3	House 4	House 5
Color	Yellow	Blue	Red	Ivory	Green
Nationality	Norwegian	Ukrainian	Englishman	Spaniard	Japanese
Drink	Water	Tea	Milk	Orange juice	Coffee
Cigarette	Kools	Chesterfields	Old Gold	Lucky Strike	Parliaments
Pet	Fox	Horse	Snails	Dog	Zebra

President Kennedy supposedly solved this riddle in less than an hour while the CEO of a Fortune 500 company recently took more than 2 hours to solve it. The best time I know of is 19 minutes, which was how long my friend Aziz Moolji took to solve it. Aziz is an investment banker at Goldman Sachs.

Brett Kenefick, a classmate of mine at Harvard Business School, asked me this puzzle when we were both still analysts at Goldman Sachs.

Tricky Twenty #16

Answer: 55. 1597. It is the (nth $+$ 1) term in the Fibonacci sequence.

This puzzle can be solved by several methods. For a small number of steps, it can be solved by simple brute force. But that solution method becomes obsolete as the number of steps gets large. The puzzle can also be solved by extensive use of combinations, permutations, and sums. However, this is a very mathematical approach and has a high probability of error (since many computations are involved). If such a solution is desired, contact me at ksrinivas@mba2001.hbs.edu. However, the more elegant solution uses backwards induction.

Let's solve for the nine-step situation. What is the last possible action that can be done to arrive at the ninth step? It can either be a single step (coming from the eighth step) or it can be a double step (coming from the seventh step). So, it should be evident that the number of ways to get to the ninth step is simply the sum of the number of ways to get to the eighth step plus the number of ways to get to the seventh step. In other words,

# of ways to 9th step = # of ways to 8th step + # of ways to 7th step

There is a little subtlety here. It is true that from the seventh step, you can take a single step to the eighth step and then again take another single step. However, this batch of sequences is already counted in the portion labeled "# of ways to the 8th step." Hence, there is no double-counting (which some people argue) because this batch of sequences is only counted in "# of ways to the 8th step" and not in "# of ways to the 7th step." This allows for a simple addition, since there is a one-to-one mapping from either the seventh step or the eighth step to the ninth step.

Now, roll the analysis further back. How can you get to the eighth step? Obviously, it is just the sum of the number of ways to the seventh step plus the number of ways to the sixth step. Likewise, to count the ways to get to the seventh step, you just sum the number of ways to the sixth step plus the number of ways to the fifth step. This type of number sequence, where each term is the sum of the preceding two terms, is the Fibonacci sequence.

The first twenty terms of the Fibonacci sequence are: 1, 1, 2, 3, 5, 8, 13, 21, 34, 55, 89, 144, 233, 377, 610, 987, 1597, 2584, 4181, and 6765. The reason that the solution is the nth $+$ 1 term, not the nth term, is that by definition the Fibonacci sequence begins with 1, 1 (the number 1 has to occur twice to start the Fibonacci sequence). This explains the nth $+$ 1 term solution. If you are not fully convinced, use simple trial-and-error for a small number of steps, which should empirically convince you.

Abhi Shilla, a doctorate student in computer science at MIT, recently asked me this riddle at a wedding.

Tricky Twenty #17

Answer: Bill's probability of winning is 16/36 (approximately 44.4%).

This is a very surprising answer: Bill gets to select his die first (from the outcome of the coin toss), but he has a less than 50% chance of winning. In fact, it is irrelevant which die Bill chooses, because regardless of Bill's choice, Warren can always select a die that gives him a 20/36 chance of winning. Specifically, if Bill selects red, Warren selects white. If Bill selects white, Warren selects blue. If Bill selects blue, Warren selects red.

I will present one scenario to show Bill's chance of winning is only 16/36. It is easy to reconstruct the other scenarios to verify that each situation leads to the same outcome. Assume Bill chooses red and Warren then chooses white. The following table shows when Bill (B) wins and when Warren (W) wins.

Bill's die	7	4	18	3	17	8
5	B	W	B	W	B	B
13	W	W	B	W	B	W
10	W	W	B	W	B	W
9	W	W	B	W	B	W
14	W	W	B	W	B	W
6	B	W	B	W	B	B

(Left label: Warren's die)

In the 36 equally likely outcomes, Bill wins 16 times and Warren wins 20 times. A similar chart can be created for when Bill selects white or blue, and then Warren selects intelligently. So Bill only has a 16/36 chance of winning even though he selects the first die.

I devised this puzzle a few years ago. I did this after reading an article which discussed the occasion when Warren Buffet showed Bill Gates three dice (all with the same total), asked Bill Gates to choose a die, then chose a die himself, and then offered to bet on who could roll a higher number. Bill Gates declined the bet. The article did not mention the numbers on the three dice, but I was able to use simple math techniques to create three dice that mimicked those in the article (i.e., having a triangular relationship in which there is always a die superior to the first die selected).

This theme—no dominant force among multiple forces—is often encountered in real life, most notably in elections. It is possible that in a three-candidate race, the people prefer A to B, prefer B to C, and prefer C to A.

When this happens, each candidate is more popular than one opponent, but less popular than another opponent. This is similar to this puzzle, in which each die is stronger than another die, but also weaker than another die.

Tricky Twenty #18

Answer: By using a simple algorithm.

I have seen many attempted solutions to this puzzle, but most of them fail for some obscure case (such as five spades or five even cards). The only solution that I know is the one described below.

From the pigeonhole principle, we know that of the five cards that Ben is given, at least two of them must be the same suit. Ben then always selects a card that has a suit that exists among the remaining four cards. To signal the suit of the card, Ben puts the other card of the same suit on top when he hands the four cards to Hillary.

To decide which of the cards from the duplicate suit to select, Bill examines the following chart:

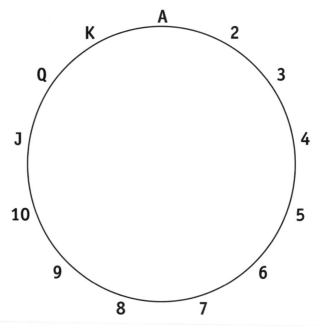

He always selects a card that is less than or equal to six steps to the right of the other card. You can empirically test all combinations to realize that regardless of the cards that are selected, there will always be a card selected that is less than or equal to six steps to the right of the other selected card. For clarity, I define right to be clockwise.

Now, label the remaining three cards high (H), middle (M), and low (L), based on some card rankings. (For example, aces are high and twos are low, and ties in value are broken by the suit order of spades, hearts, diamonds, and clubs. So the highest two cards are the ace of spades and ace of hearts and the two lowest cards are the two of diamonds and two of clubs.) There are six ways to order these three cards, namely HML, HLM, MHL, MLH, LHM, and LMH. Each of these six scenarios should represent a number from 1 to 6. This is the number that must be added to the first card passed to arrive at the desired card.

For example, assume the five cards that are given to Ben are the 6D, 3H, KS, 8C, and 7H. Then Ben would keep the 7H and pass the other four cards in the order of 3H, 8C, 6D, and KS. Instead, suppose the initial five cards are AS, KS, 7S, 3S, and 2S. Then Ben would keep the 3S and pass the other four cards in the order of 2S, AS, KS, and 7S.

Tricky Twenty #19

Answer: Yes, you can ask a question that ensures you do not marry the werewolf. You should approach the first sister and ask her, "Does the second sister lie more frequently than the third sister?"

Let us outline all of the six potential scenarios:

First sister	Second sister	Third sister	Answer
Truth-teller	Liar	Werewolf	Yes
Truth-teller	Werewolf	Liar	No
Liar	Truth-teller	Werewolf	Yes
Liar	Werewolf	Truth-teller	No
Werewolf	Truth-teller	Liar	Yes or No
Werewolf	Liar	Truth-teller	Yes or No

From the table above, we can easily derive the following marriage solution. If the first sister answers yes, then you marry the second sister. However, if the first sister answers no, then you marry the third sister. This ensures that you do not marry the werewolf.

From Brain Teaser #20, it should be apparent how simple math concepts, such as $1 \times -1 = -1 \times 1 = -1$, can be used to arrive at a seemingly complicated solution. In this puzzle, you must use the basic idea of greater than and less than to solve the puzzle. Any question that does not compare the second and third sisters will not work—you must incorporate a greater than or less than theme within the question you ask.

It should be apparent that regardless of the question you ask, you can't marry the sister you ask the question to. This is because regardless of the question you ask, you can never determine whether you are asking the werewolf or not (since she can always say yes or no).

Tricky Twenty #20

Answer: The conjecture is true. The only known proof to date is to prove by example (i.e., show that at least 95 numbers can be expressed with exactly four 4s).

Here is the full solution. To date, 73, 77, 87, 93, and 99 are still unsolvable.

$1 = 44/44$

$2 = 4/4 + 4/4$

$3 = \sqrt{4} + 4/(\sqrt{4} + \sqrt{4})$

$4 = 4/\sqrt{4} + 4/\sqrt{4}$

$5 = 4 + 4/(\sqrt{4} + \sqrt{4})$

$6 = \sqrt{4} + \sqrt{4} + 4/\sqrt{4}$

$7 = 4 + 4 - 4/4$

$8 = \sqrt{4} + \sqrt{4} + \sqrt{4} + \sqrt{4}$

$9 = 4 + 4 + 4/4$

$10 = 4 + 4 + 4/\sqrt{4}$

$11 = 4!/\sqrt{4} - 4/4$

$12 = 4!/\sqrt{4} + 4 - 4$

$13 = 4!/\sqrt{4} + 4/4$

$14 = 4!/\sqrt{4} + 4/\sqrt{4}$

$15 = 4 \times 4 - 4/4$

$16 = 4 + 4 + 4 + 4$

$17 = 4 \times 4 + 4/4$

$18 = 4 \times 4 + 4/\sqrt{4}$

$19 = 4! - 4 - 4/4$

$20 = 4 \times 4 + \sqrt{4} + \sqrt{4}$

$21 = 4! - \sqrt{4} - 4/4$

$22 = 4! - \sqrt{4} + 4 - 4$

$23 = 4! - \sqrt{4} + 4/4$

$24 = 4! + 4 - \sqrt{4} - \sqrt{4}$

$25 = 4! + \sqrt{4} - 4/4$

$26 = 4! + \sqrt{4} + 4 - 4$

$27 = 4! + \sqrt{4} + 4/4$

$28 = 4! + 4 + 4 - 4$

$29 = 4! + 4 + 4/4$

$30 = 4! + 4 + 4/\sqrt{4}$

$31 = 4! + [(4! + 4)/4]$

$32 = (4 \times 4) + (4 \times 4)$

$33 = 4! + [(4 - .4)/.4]$

$34 = 4! + 4 + 4 + \sqrt{4}$

$35 = 4! + 44/4$

$36 = 4! + 4 + 4 + 4$

$37 = 4! + [(4! + \sqrt{4})/\sqrt{4}]$

$38 = 4! + (4 \times 4) - \sqrt{4}$

$39 = 44 - \sqrt{4}/.4$

$40 = 4/.4 \times (\sqrt{4} + \sqrt{4})$

$41 = [(4 \times 4) + .4]/.4$

$42 = 44 - 4/\sqrt{4}$

$43 = 44 - 4/4$

$44 = 44 + 4 - 4$

$45 = 44 + 4/4$

$46 = 44 + 4/\sqrt{4}$

$47 = 4! + 4! - 4/4$

$48 = 4! + 4! + 4 - 4$

$49 = 4! + 4! + 4/4$

$50 = 4! + 4! + 4/\sqrt{4}$

$51 = (4! - 4 + .4)/.4$

$52 = 4! + 4! + \sqrt{4} + \sqrt{4}$

$53 = (4! - \sqrt{4})/.4 - \sqrt{4}$

$54 = 44 + 4/.4$

$55 = [4! - (4/\sqrt{4})]/.4$

$56 = 4! + 4! + 4 + 4$

$57 = (4! + .4)/.4 - 4$

$58 = (4! - .4 - .4)/.4$

$59 = [(\sqrt{4} + \sqrt{4})! - .4]/.4$

$60 = 4!/.4 - 4 + 4$

$61 = 4!/.4 + 4/4$

$62 = 4!/.4 + 4/\sqrt{4}$

$63 = (4! - .4)/.4 + 4$

$64 = 4 \times 4 \times (\sqrt{4} + \sqrt{4})$

$65 = [4! + (4/\sqrt{4})]/.4$

$66 = (4! + .4 + \sqrt{4})/.4$

$67 = (4! + \sqrt{4})/.4 + \sqrt{4}$

$68 = 4 \times 4 \times 4 + 4$

$69 = (4! + \sqrt{4})/.4 + 4$

$70 = (4! + \sqrt{4} + \sqrt{4})/.4$

$71 = (4! + 4 + .4)/.4$

$72 = 44 + 4 + 4!$

$73 = ***$

$74 = (4! + 4)/.4 + 4$

$75 = (4! + 4 + \sqrt{4})/.4$

$76 = 4!/.4 + (4 \times 4)$

$77 = ***$

$78 = (4! - 4) \times 4 - \sqrt{4}$

$79 = (4! - \sqrt{4})/.4 + 4!$

$80 = 4!/.4 + 4! - 4$

$81 = [(4 - .4)/.4]*\sqrt{4}$

$82 = 4!/.4 + 4! - \sqrt{4}$

$83 = (4! - .4)/.4 + 4!$

$84 = 4!/.4 + (\sqrt{4} + \sqrt{4})!$

$85 = (4! + .4)/.4 + 4!$

$86 = 4! \times 4 - 4/.4$

$87 = ***$

$88 = 4! \times 4 - 4 - 4$

$89 = (4! + \sqrt{4})/.4 + 4!$

$90 = 4! \times 4 - 4 - \sqrt{4}$

$91 = 4! \times 4 - \sqrt{4}/.4$

$92 = 4! \times 4 - \sqrt{4} - \sqrt{4}$

$93 = ***$

$94 = 4! \times 4 - 4 + \sqrt{4}$

$95 = 4! \times 4 - 4/4$

$96 = 4! \times 4 + 4 - 4$

$97 = 4! \times 4 + 4/4$

$98 = 4! \times 4 + 4 - \sqrt{4}$

$99 = ***$

$100 = (4! + 4/4) \times 4$

I created this puzzle myself one day when I was very bored in marketing class. I will award a $1,000 prize to the first one who is able to solve for one of the five remaining numbers. Just e-mail me at ksrinivas@ mba2001.hbs.edu with your solution.

Books Available From Robert D. Reed Publishers

Please include payment with orders. Send indicated book/s to:

Name:_____

Address:_____

City:_____ State:_____ Zip:_____

Phone:(____)_____ E-mail:_____

Titles and Authors	Unit Price
____ *Brain Teasers* by Kiran Srinivas	$9.95
____ *Gotta Minute? The ABC's of Successful Living* by Tom Massey, Ph.D., N.D.	9.95
____ *Gotta Minute? Practical Tips for Abundant Living:* *The ABC's of Total Health* by Tom Massey, Ph.D., N.D.	9.95
____ *Gotta Minute? How to Look & Feel Great!* by Marcia F. Kamph, M.S., D.C.	11.95
____ *Gotta Minute? Yoga for Health, Relaxation &* *Well-being* by Nirvair Singh Khalsa	9.95
____ *Gotta Minute? Ultimate Guide of One-Minute* *Workouts for Anyone, Anywhere, Anytime!* by Bonnie Nygard, M.Ed. & Bonnie Hopper, M.Ed.	9.95
____ *A Kid's Herb Book for Children of All Ages* by Lesley Tierra, Acupuncturist and Herbalist	19.95
____ *House Calls: How we can all heal the world* *one visit at a time* by Patch Adams, M.D.	11.95
____ *500 Tips for Coping with Chronic Illness* by Pamela D. Jacobs, M.A.	11.95

Enclose a copy of this order form with payment for books. Send to the address below. Shipping & handling: $2.50 for first book plus $1.00 for each additional book. California residents add 8.5% sales tax. We offer discounts for large orders.

Please make checks payable to: **Robert D. Reed Publishers.**

Total enclosed: $_____. See our website for more books!

Robert D. Reed Publishers
750 La Playa, Suite 647, San Francisco, CA 94121
Phone: 650-994-6570 • Fax: 650-994-6579
Email: 4bobreed@msn.com • www.rdrpublishers.com